AF606750

Sabine Moritz
HELICOPTER

with a poem by Adam Zagajewski

HENI PUBLISHING LONDON

Helicopter

'I am not indifferent to the fact
that this piece exists in its own right,
even if no-one is there. … These pieces exist.'
Karlheinz Stockhausen

Sabine Moritz often works in series, as she engages with certain themes over a period of years. She returns to individual motifs, painting and drawing them anew, varying them and re-interpreting them or portraying them in different atmospheres, yet always ensuring that they are still recognisable. The motifs and themes in these series arise from her subjective observations. In conversation she has specifically referred to the value of 'taking one's own life as an example and working through the things that are closest to one'. In her case this has led, among other things, to flower compositions – roses and lilies – to architectural drawings from memory and to the *Helicopter* series. In a wider sense, however, her works are about something with a much broader relevance than merely the individual observations of one artist: they are about the relationship of memory, the culture of memory and cultural remembrance. Her series achieve this objective, more general dimension through the persistent repetition and transfer of a particular motif into different (memory) realms. Sabine Moritz's works heighten our awareness of memory as a dynamic process in which things are constantly reframed and where there can be no definitive picture of the past. Her drawings and paintings capture remembered images in a way that also conveys a clear sense of the transience of memory.

Her earliest works of this kind arose from her spontaneous, personal recollections of the environs of her childhood and youth in Lobeda, a suburb of high-rise concrete buildings on the outskirts of Jena in the then GDR, where she lived from 1973 to 1981, before moving into the city of Jena in 1981. In 1985 her family emigrated to West Germany, where Sabine Moritz started to study art in 1989. And it was only after this, in 1991, that she started to draw, from memory, urban scenes from her childhood. Yet however much these drawings provide access to those reminiscences, their often blurred, searching, erased and smudged lines also attest to the deep impenetrability of memory. These first works were published in the book *Lobeda* (2010); a second group of works on the same subject, done in 1992–94, have been published in *Jena – Düsseldorf* (2012).

In 2002 Sabine Moritz made the first of her *Helicopters*, at a time of radical change in almost every aspect of life, following the events of 11 September 2001. Those attacks, whose perpetrators had also used violent imagery as a weapon, both transformed the meaning of existing symbols and created entirely new symbols. 'Aircraft have now also come to symbolise loss. They have become an ambivalent symbol. Aeroplanes were once perfectly ordinary objects, but since 9/11 they have also taken on another meaning.' The symbolic meaning of helicopters has also changed, albeit over a longer period of time. Helicopters are generally used in war zones where the terrain prevents larger aircraft from landing.

During the Vietnam War helicopters came into their own as an important means of attack and the many press and television images of their deployment ensured that to this day they still stand as a symbol of the brutality of war.

In recent years Sabine Moritz has addressed the motif of war in her works. Like the helicopters, whose presence in her works ensues solely from her interest in the shift in their symbolic meaning, the scenes of war depicted by Sabine Moritz are not intended as representations of historical fact. If anything these works are the outcome of her interest in the impact of war on our culture and on our culture of memory. For Sabine Moritz there is an enduring connection with earlier wars, and she feels an acute 'sense of awareness that we are all actually living in a postwar era. Even if we never think about it, we are nevertheless surrounded by the consequences of war. The last war changed so many things and still lives on in the present.' Moritz is referring here not only to the memories in people's minds, but also to those that are inscribed into our cities today, in the form of the postwar architecture that created entirely new cityscapes and the monuments and places of remembrance that she has also focused on in her work for some time now.

In recent decades helicopters have variously appeared as motifs in works of art. In the 1970s artists such as Nancy Spero and Martha Rosler created series that referred directly to the Vietnam War and used their art to comment on the often falsified or one-sided reporting on the war in the news media. In Nancy Spero's drawings *War Series* (1966-70) military helicopters almost become living flying-objects, which – as killing machines – spit out their victims like bombs, as she once said to me in an interview. At the same time as these artists were producing their anti-war series, the French photographer Robert Doisneau took his shot of *The Helicopters* (1972). This was not primarily a protest against war but rather juxtaposes the motif of the human body – here seen in the form of the sculpture of the *Three Graces* made by Aristide Maillol in 1938 – with that of the helicopter, as a group of four flying in formation in the sky above the sculpture and as a technological achievement whose appearance is generally associated with an event of some kind. Andy Warhol, whose art frequently drew on events in daily life captured by the media, focussed on the use of helicopters in emergencies (*Emergency Helicopter*, 1983). John Baldessari, for his part, highlighted the insect-like appearance of these aircraft in *Helicopter and Insects (one red)* (1990). The sound of rotor blades is quite unmistakable, and often heard before the helicopter itself comes into view. Steve McQueen exploited this in his video *Static* (2009), in which the camera circles around the Statue of Liberty to the deafening sound of the helicopter from which it was filmed. In one of his last works, the *Helicopter String Quartet* (1992–93), Karlheinz Stockhausen even used the sound of helicopter blades as a second set of instruments. Stockhausen himself commented that 'some music can make us forget ourselves, it can cause us to temporarily depart from normal physiological time or bodily time'. This departure from time is also evident in the works by Sabine Moritz – although they have been made in an era when the events of 9/11 have ensured that the meaning of old symbols have been altered and new symbols have come into being.

Sabine Moritz's images of helicopters have almost all arisen from her interest in this shift in their symbolic meaning and not as a consequence of a particular event. The source materials for many of these compositions are drawn from her archive of newspaper photographs. And although some of the works have quite specific titles (such as *Baghdad II*, 2004), once the image has been detached from its original context it can no longer be associated with a particular event and comes instead to represent the theme as a whole. The rendering of these images in drawings and paintings thus becomes a commentary on the wider portrayal of war and military force. At the same time, however, Sabine Moritz also personifies the image of the helicopter in some works, which are based on a detailed study of the nature of a helicopter: 'Helicopters are more active, they appear more autonomous and less contemplative than aeroplanes. They can fly in any direction, they can suddenly loom into view and disappear again… As symbols they are much more versatile. If aircraft were fish, helicopters would be amphibians.' In one composition (*Roses*, 2005) the helicopters even become insects circling around the roses, and in another the helicopter takes the form of a strange, mythical creature with something akin to facial features (*Schöner Helikopter I*, 2009). The impact of these helicopter pictures arises from the fact that a subject that is familiar to us all from images in newspapers and on television has been transferred into the artist's own language of drawing and painting, which ranges from documentary depictions of a helicopter performing an emergency landing (*Notlandung*, 2004) to playfully poetic compositions. The objective nature of these works, which is highlighted by the principle of seriality, is at the same time countered by the atmospheric nature of their depiction.

For the artist herself the helicopters have a wide variety of meanings, all of which derive from the same motif. In a letter to Adam Zagajewski she remarked that 'the helicopters are perhaps odd metaphors that carry us far away. A big empty space. Sometimes they are symbols for the Self, sometimes for the Other and sometimes they tell a story.' The dynamic process in the series ensues from the changes in the sizes and colours of the helicopter motifs and in their surroundings: things are constantly varied and there is no ultimately definitive image. Looking back at the history of art and of the press and media, the significance of the helicopter has long been a factor in our collective memory of cultural images. The artistic tension in Moritz's series arises from the fine balance of wider meaning and subjective response.

Hans Ulrich Obrist

1 Evening I, 2007

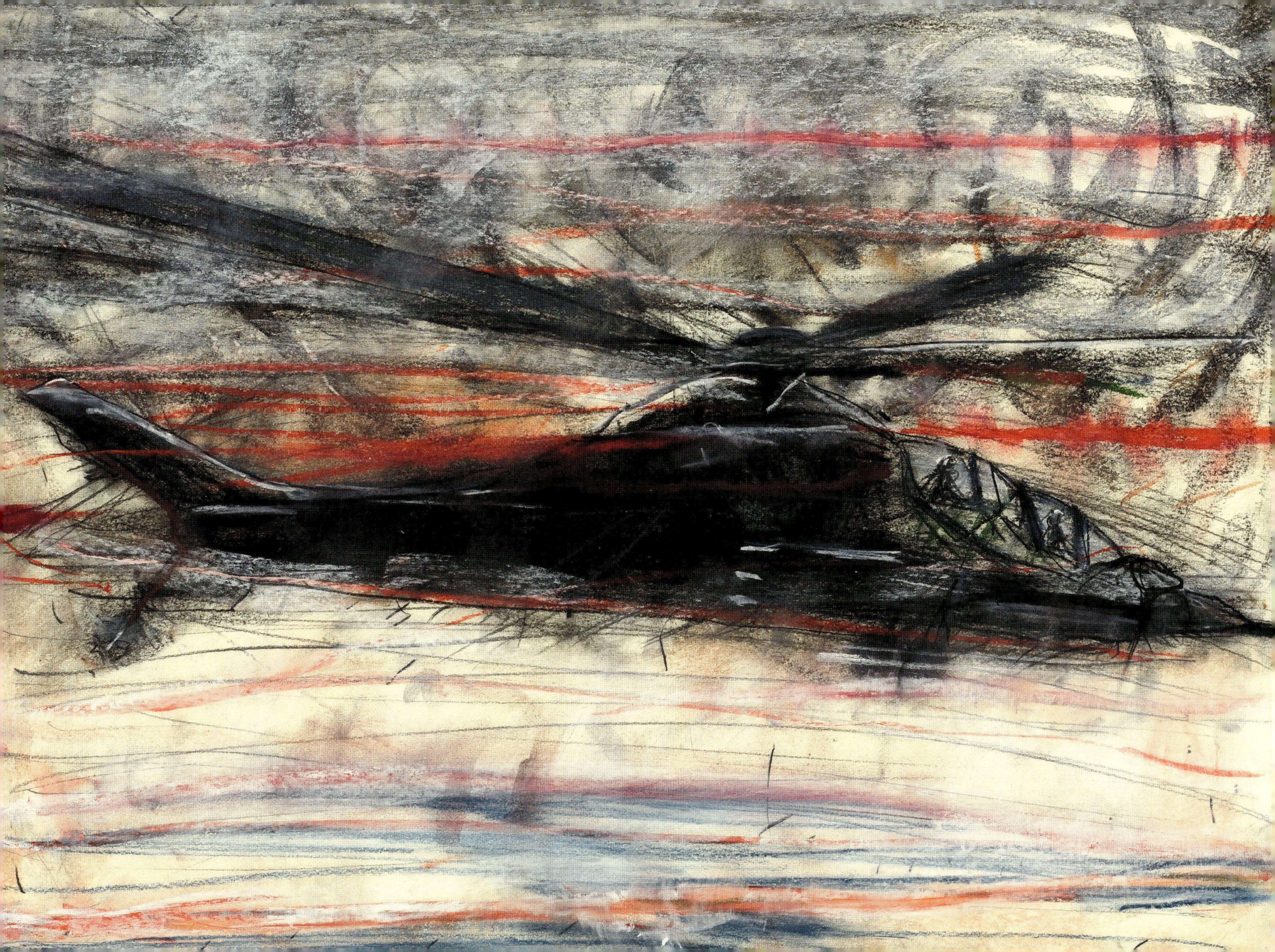

Evening II, 2009

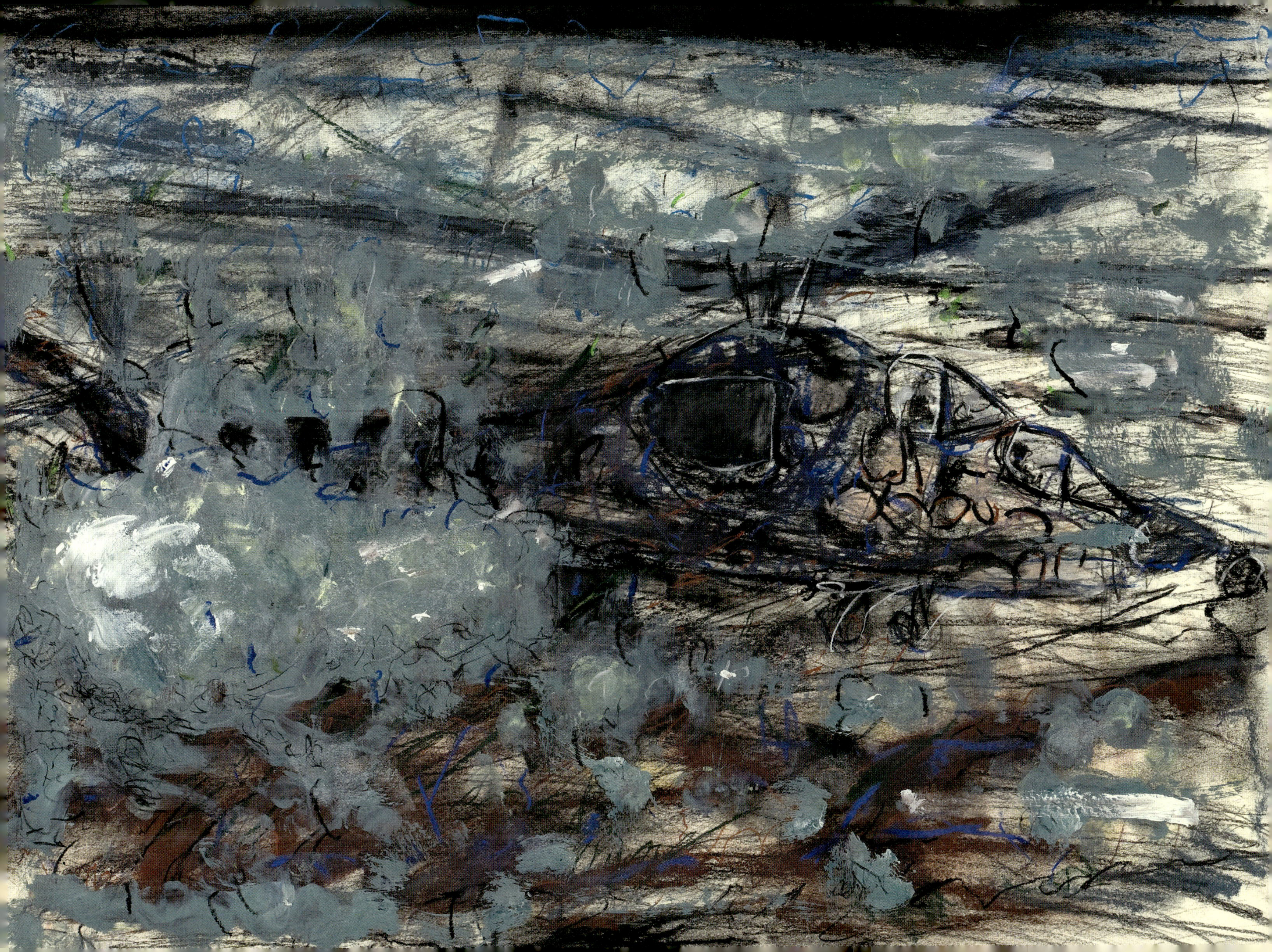

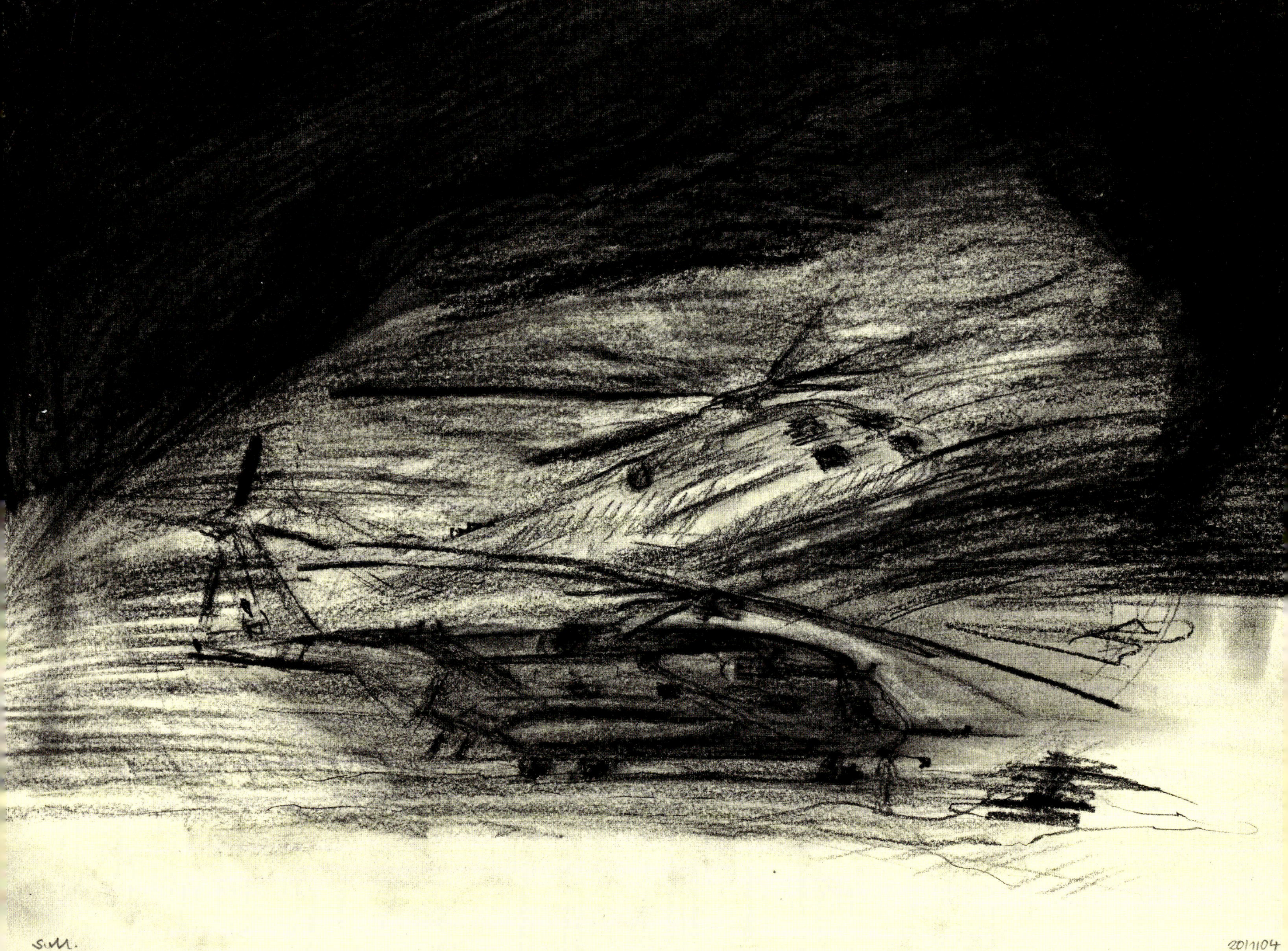
S.M.
20/11/04

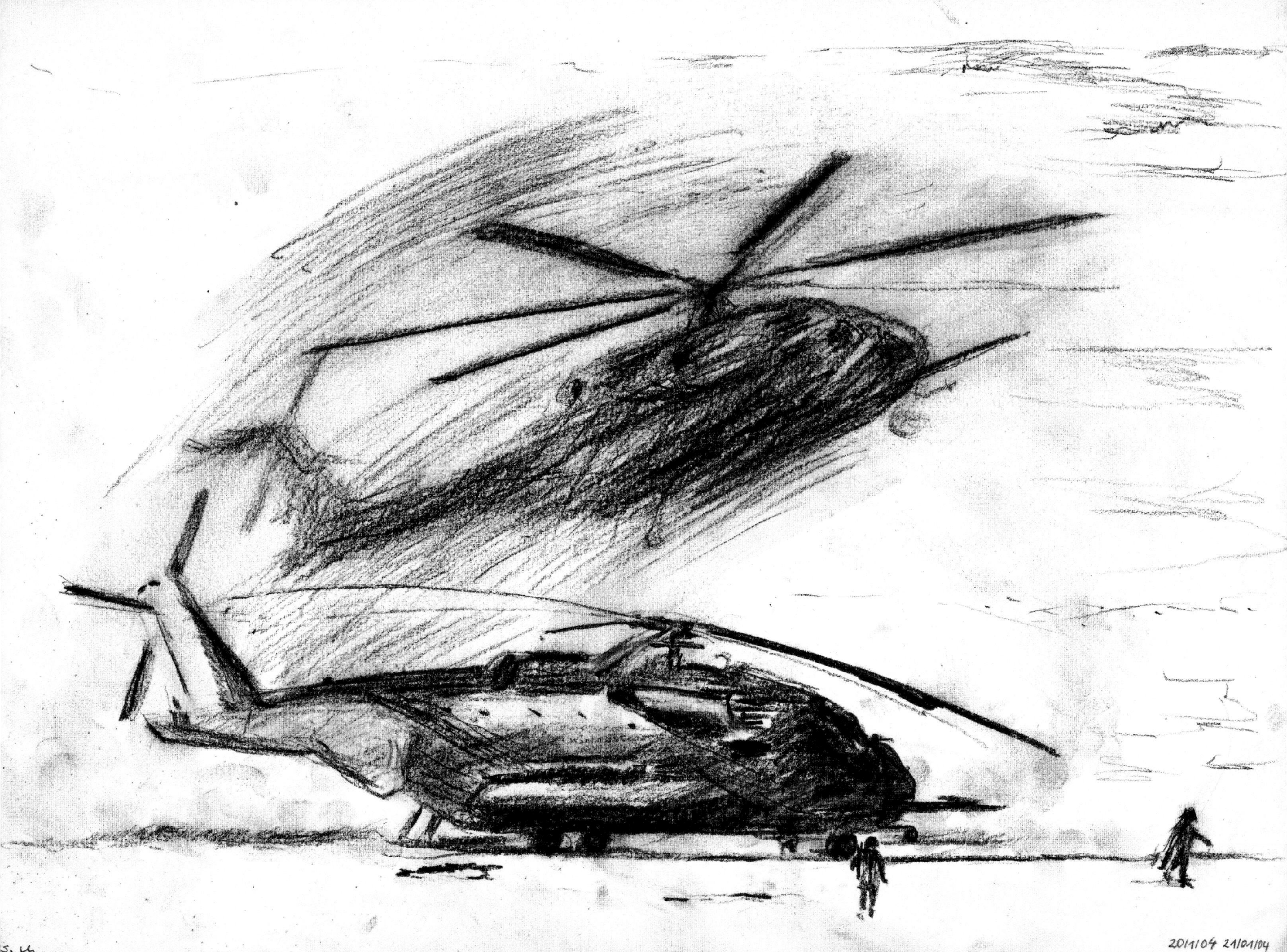
S. M.
20/1/04 21/01/04

3 Start Night, 2004

4 Start Day, 2004

5 Kandahar, 2004

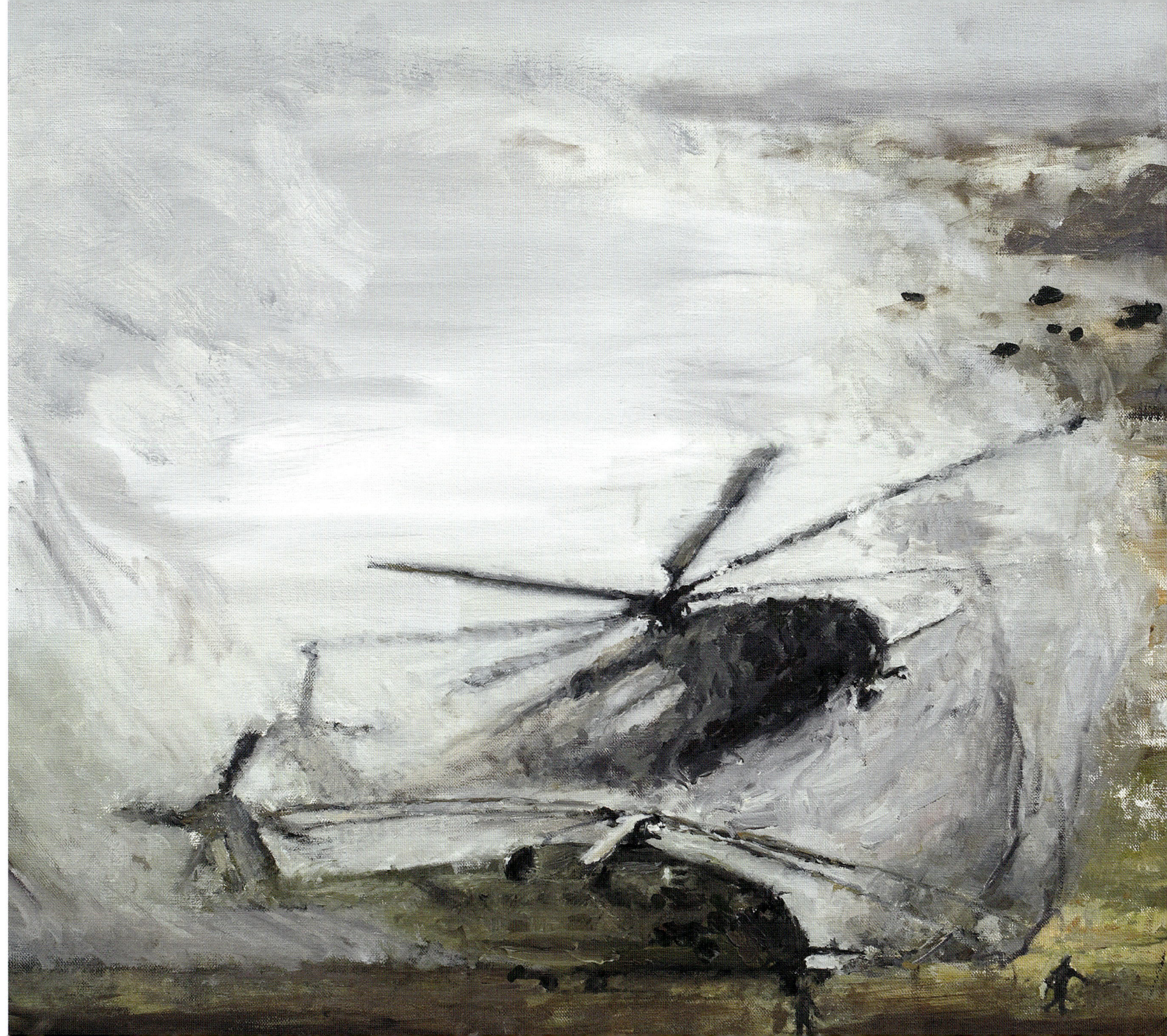

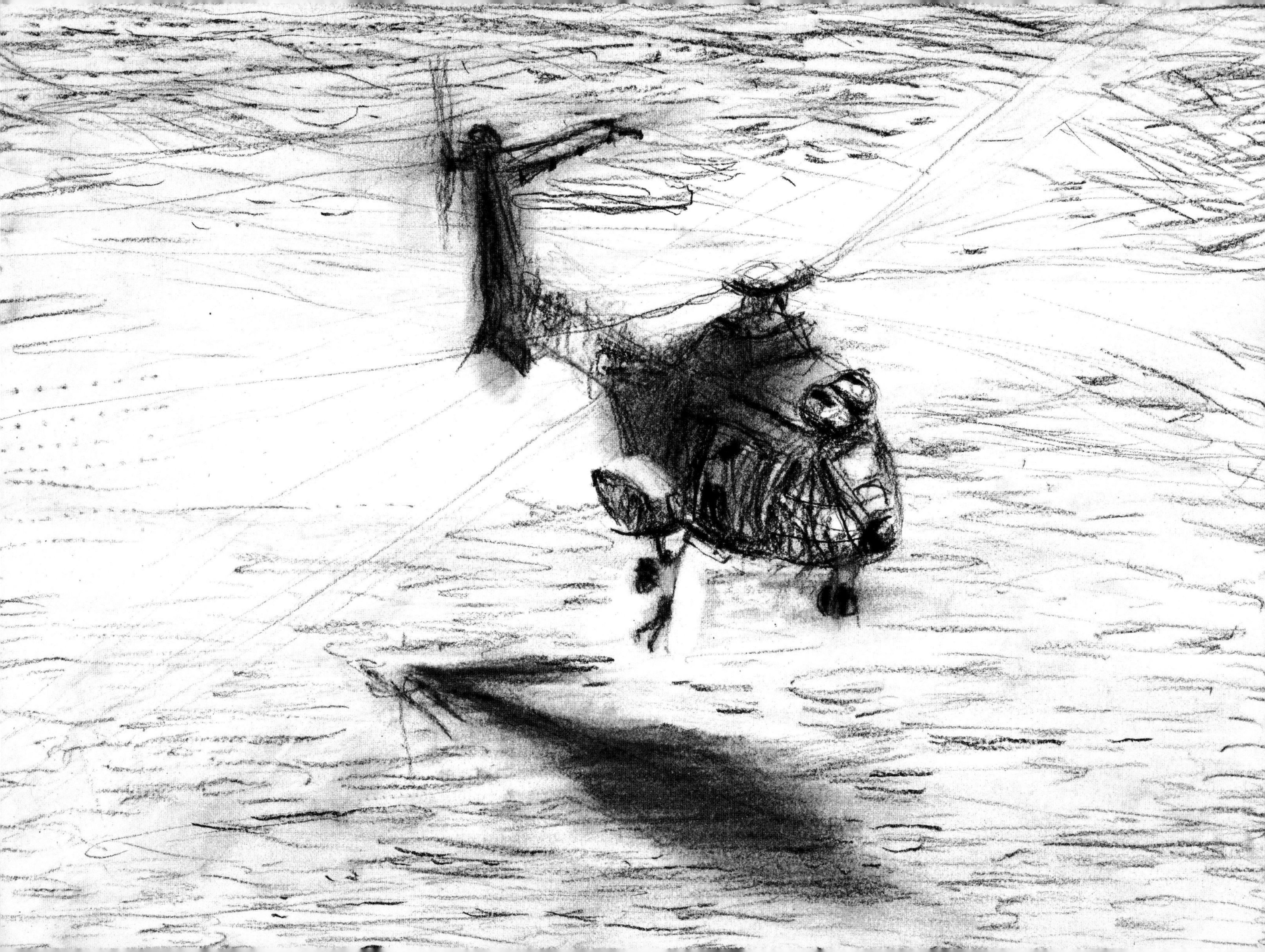

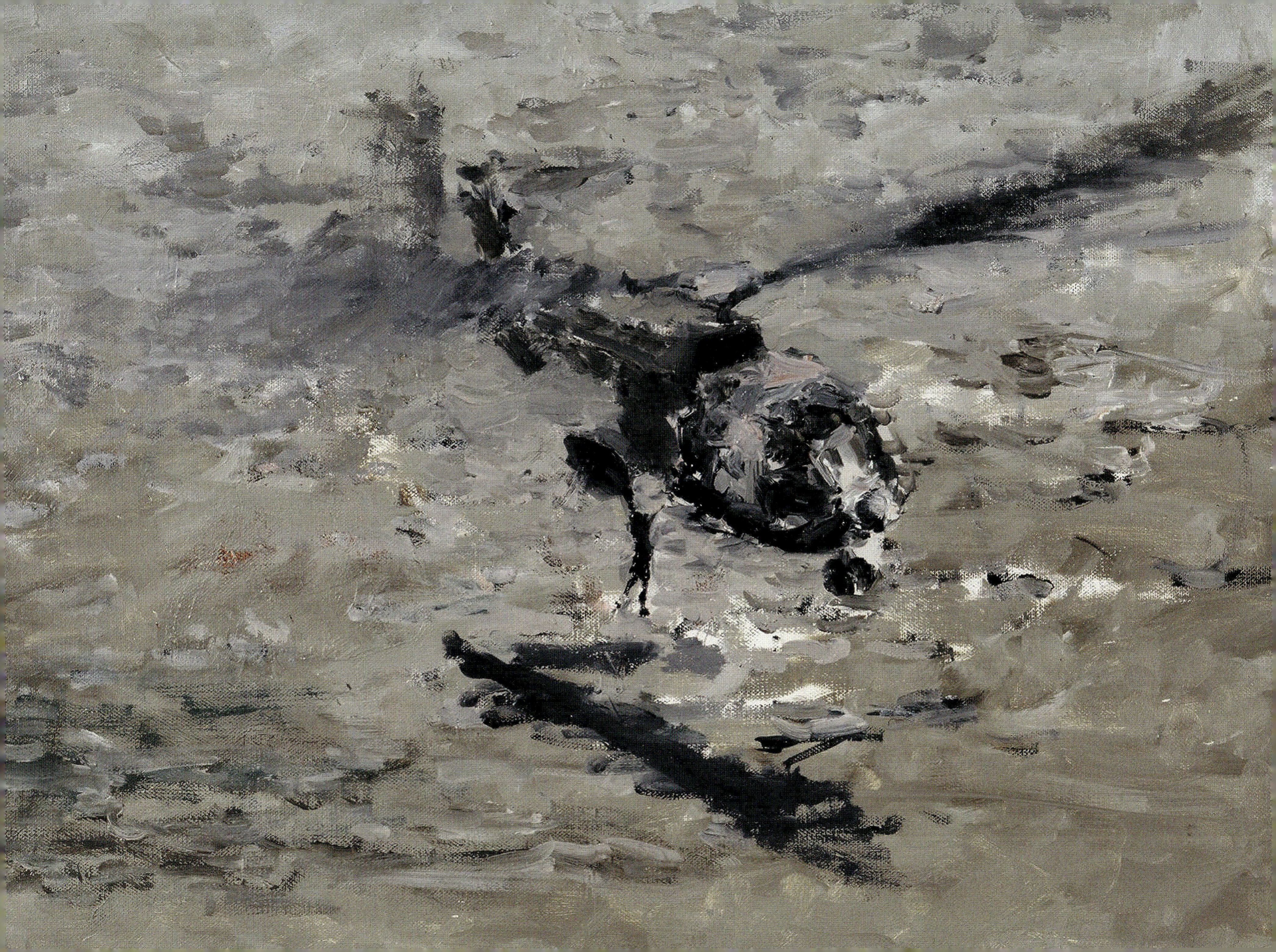

6 Saving Action (Flood), 2004

7 Flood, 2004

8 Baghdad, 2004

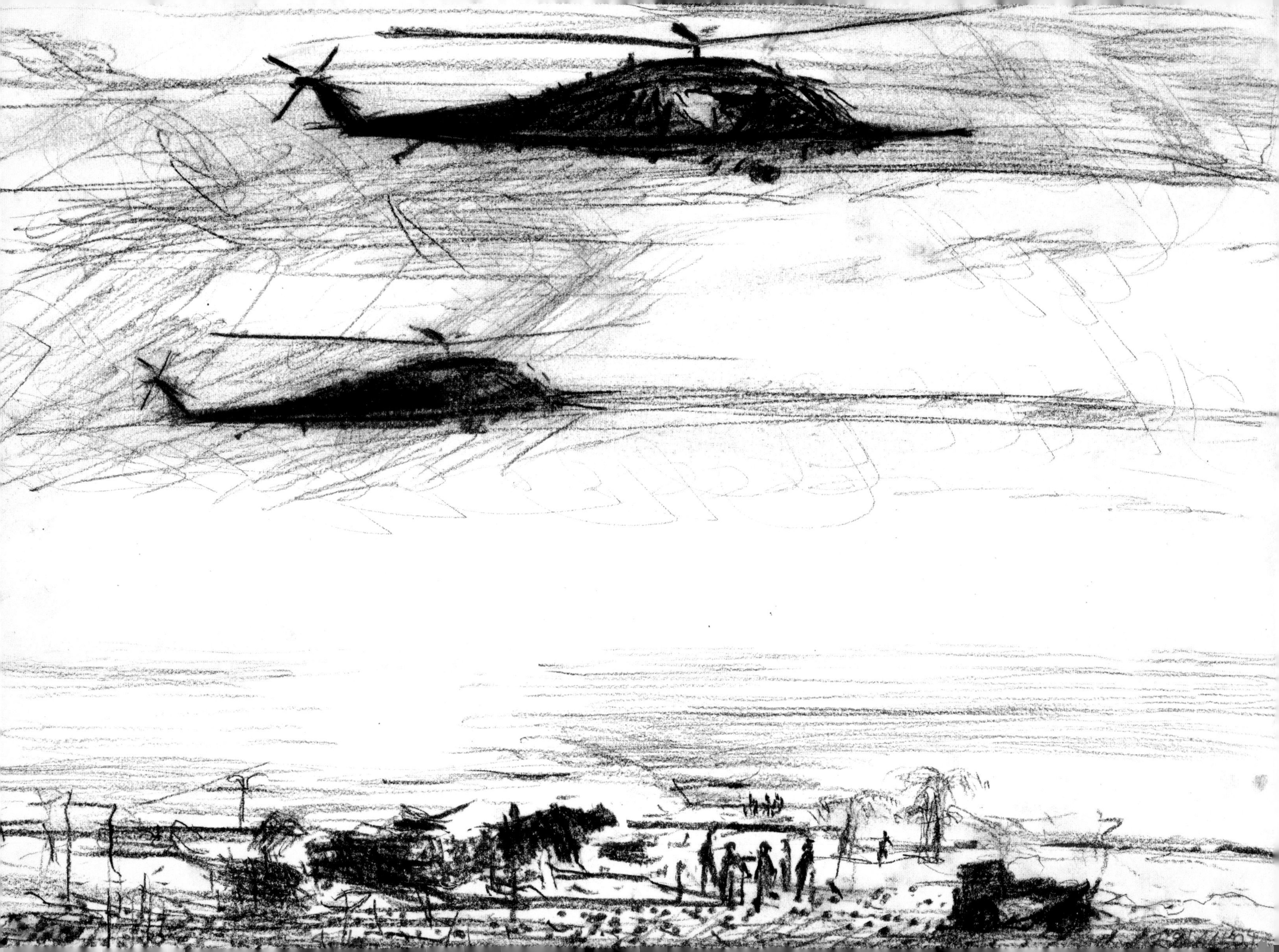

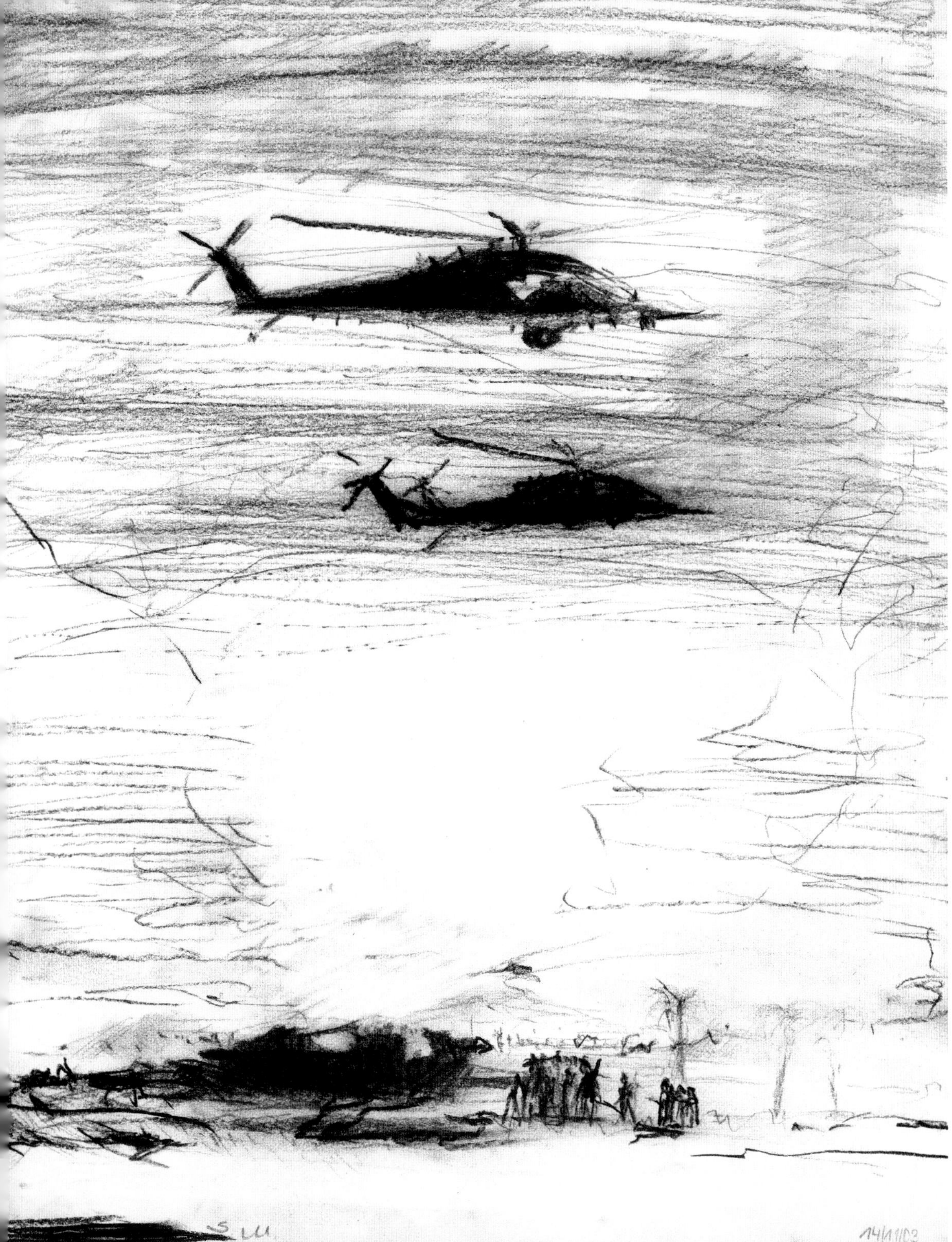

9 Baghdad II, 2003

Iron ships

Eugène Delacroix had been watching
the steam ships on the English Channel,
which slowly but systematically were starting
to push out the frigates with their swollen, snow-white sails
and wrote with regret in his diary:
everything around us undergoes decline,
the beauty of the world departs forever,
incessantly there keep appearing new
inventions, maybe they're useful,
but they're infinitely boring
(such as the iron railroads,
locomotives heavy as a headsman's hand).
While he painted handsome horses and furious lions
and their muscles tensed under their short coats,
and the uniforms of spahis, plenty of red, which
blood can give or exotic fabrics,
and the light dancing on a saber's blade
– and then all that was left were machines,
grey machines and splashes of oil
on the sand, on sawdust (and also blood).
There is plenty of the new reality
and what was marvelous has now become shy,
it's hard to track down, to remember,
to record, and yet soaring,
white, multi-storey clouds,
proud and arrogant cumulus, go sailing
over France, over Germany, over Poland,
they go sailing over us and hiding within them
are loyal migratory birds, the cranes and finches,
living in them are swallows, orioles and swifts,
and also airborne iron ships,
which either kill us or save us.
Ever hovering over us are
death and salvation.

Żelazne statki

Eugène Delacroix przyglądał się
na Kanale La Manche statkom parowym,
które powoli, systematycznie zaczęły
wypierać fregaty o wydętych białych żaglach
i pisał ze smutkiem w swoim dzienniku:
wszystko wokół nas ulega degradacji,
piękno świata odchodzi na zawsze;
nieprzerwanie pojawiają się nowe
wynalazki, być może użyteczne,
lecz nieskończenie banalne
(na przykład koleje żelazne,
lokomotywy ciężkie jak ręka kata).
On sam malował dorodne konie i groźne lwy
i ich muskuły napięte pod krótką sierścią,
i mundury spahisów, dużo czerwieni, którą
może dać krew albo egzotyczne tkaniny,
i światło tańczące na klindze szabli
– a potem zostały już tylko maszyny,
szare maszyny i plamy oleju
na piasku, na trocinach (i także krew).
Jest dużo nowej rzeczywistości
i to, co cudowne stało się nieśmiałe,
trudno je odnaleźć, zapamiętać,
utrwalić, a jednak wysokie,
białe, wielopiętrowe chmury,
aroganckie, dumne cumulusy, płyną
nad Francją i nad Niemcami i nad Polską,
płyną nad nami i kryją się w nich
wierne ptaki wędrowne, żurawie i gile,
mieszkają w nich jaskółki, wilgi, jerzyki,
i także żelazne statki powietrzne,
które nas zabijają lub ratują.
Wciąż krążą nad nami
śmierć i ocalenie.

Adam Zagajewski, 2014

 Crash Landing I, 2004

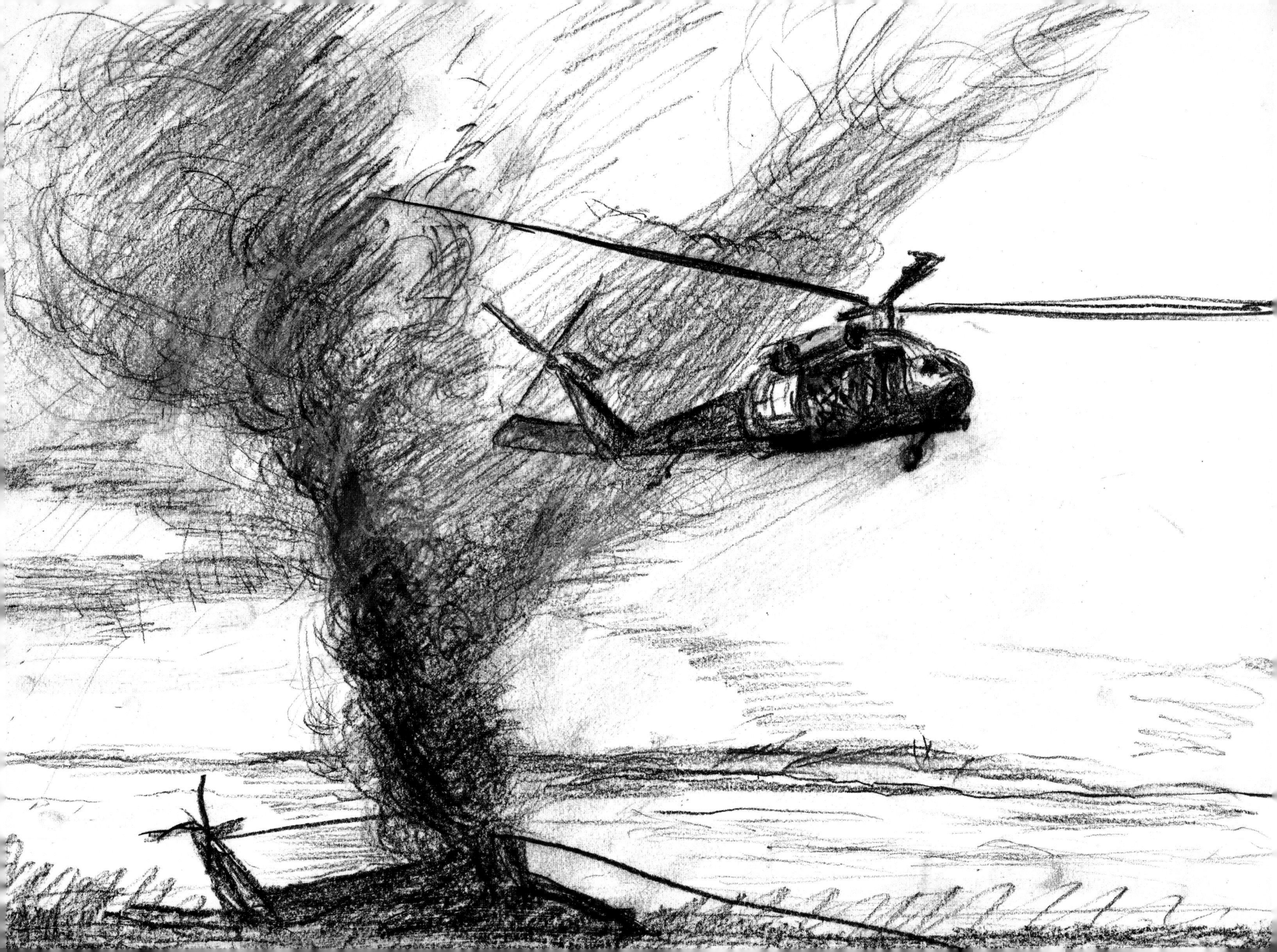

11 Crash Landing II, 2004

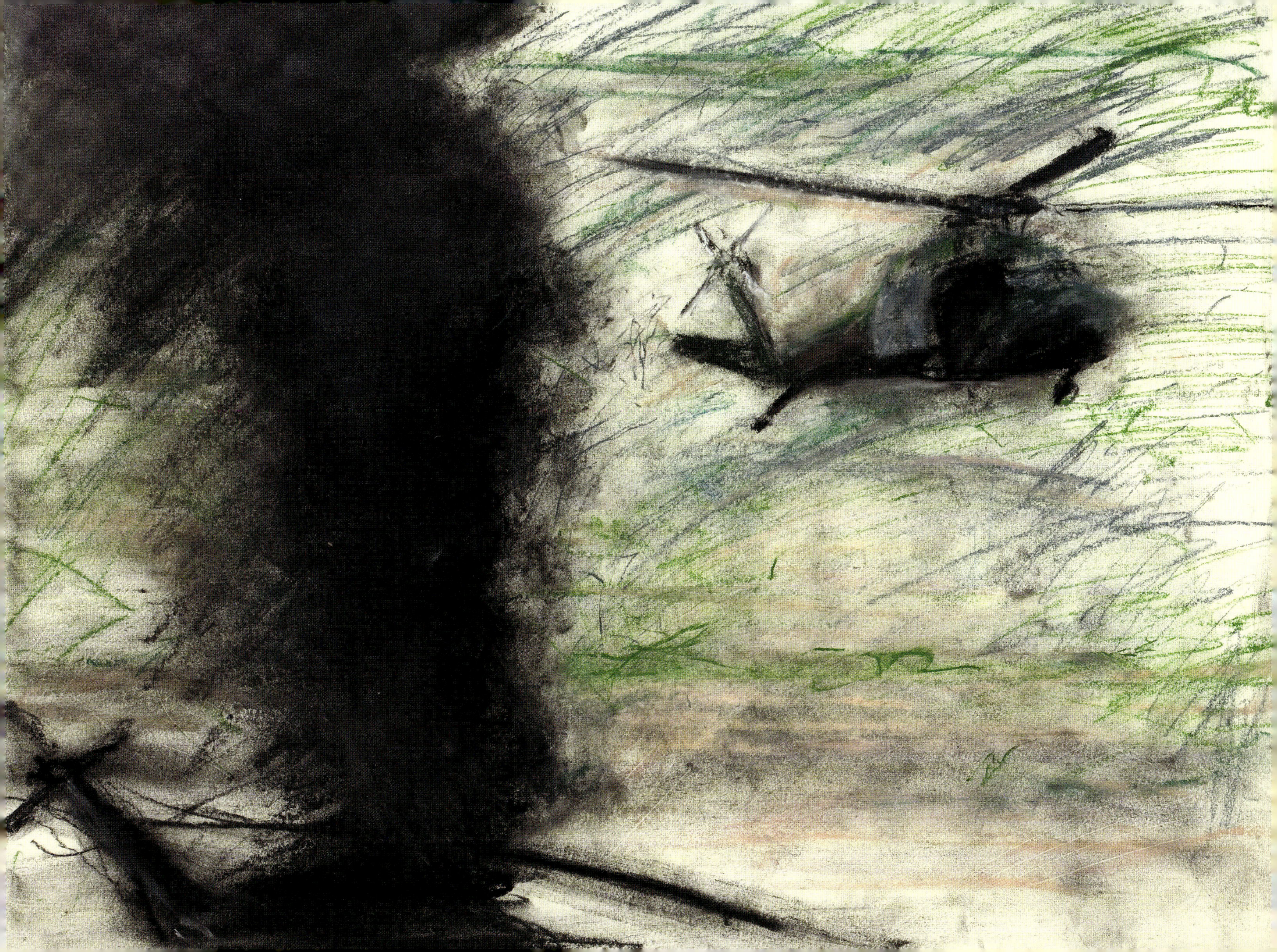

 Crash Landing III, 2004

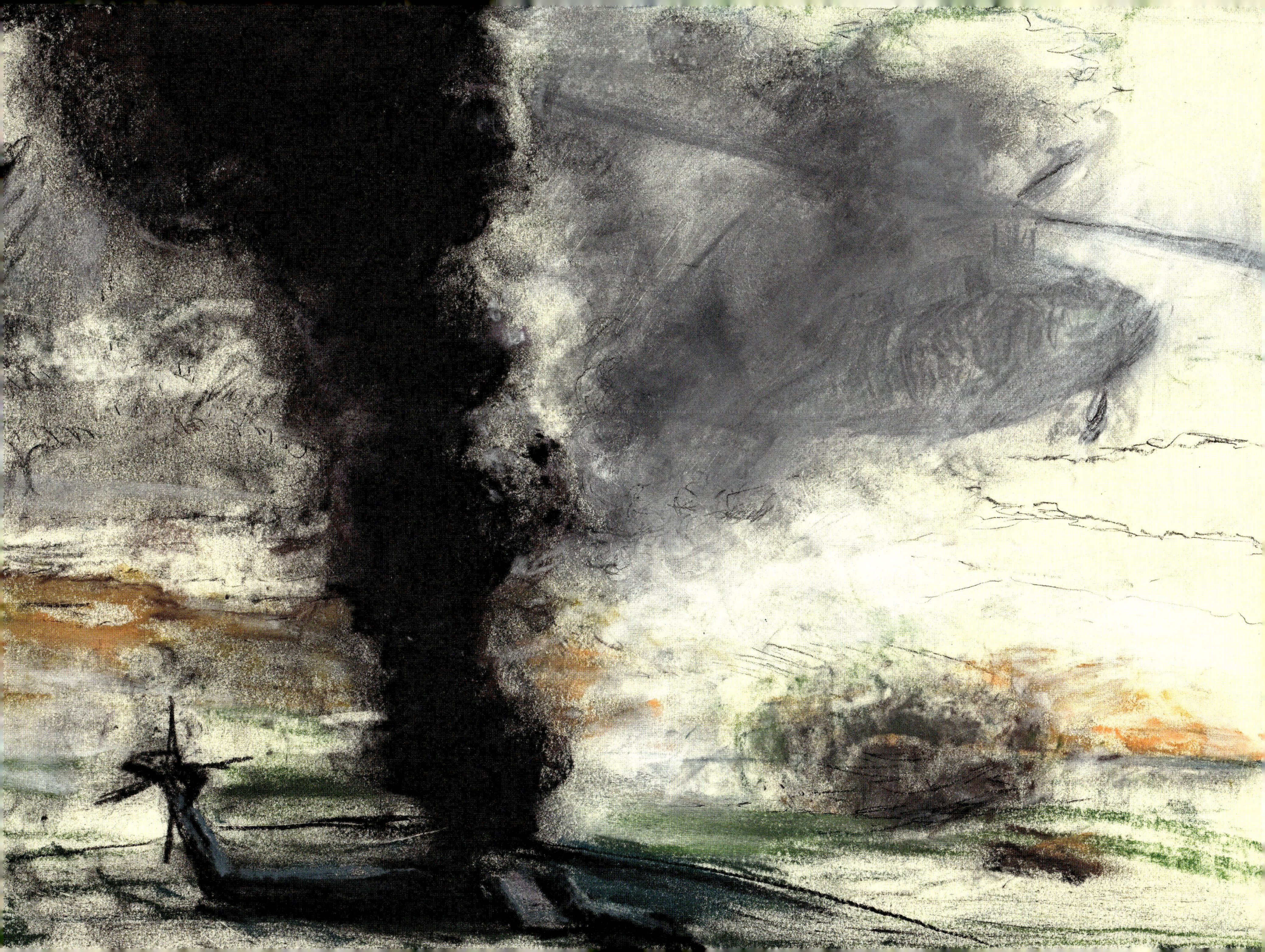

13 Crash Landing IV, 2004

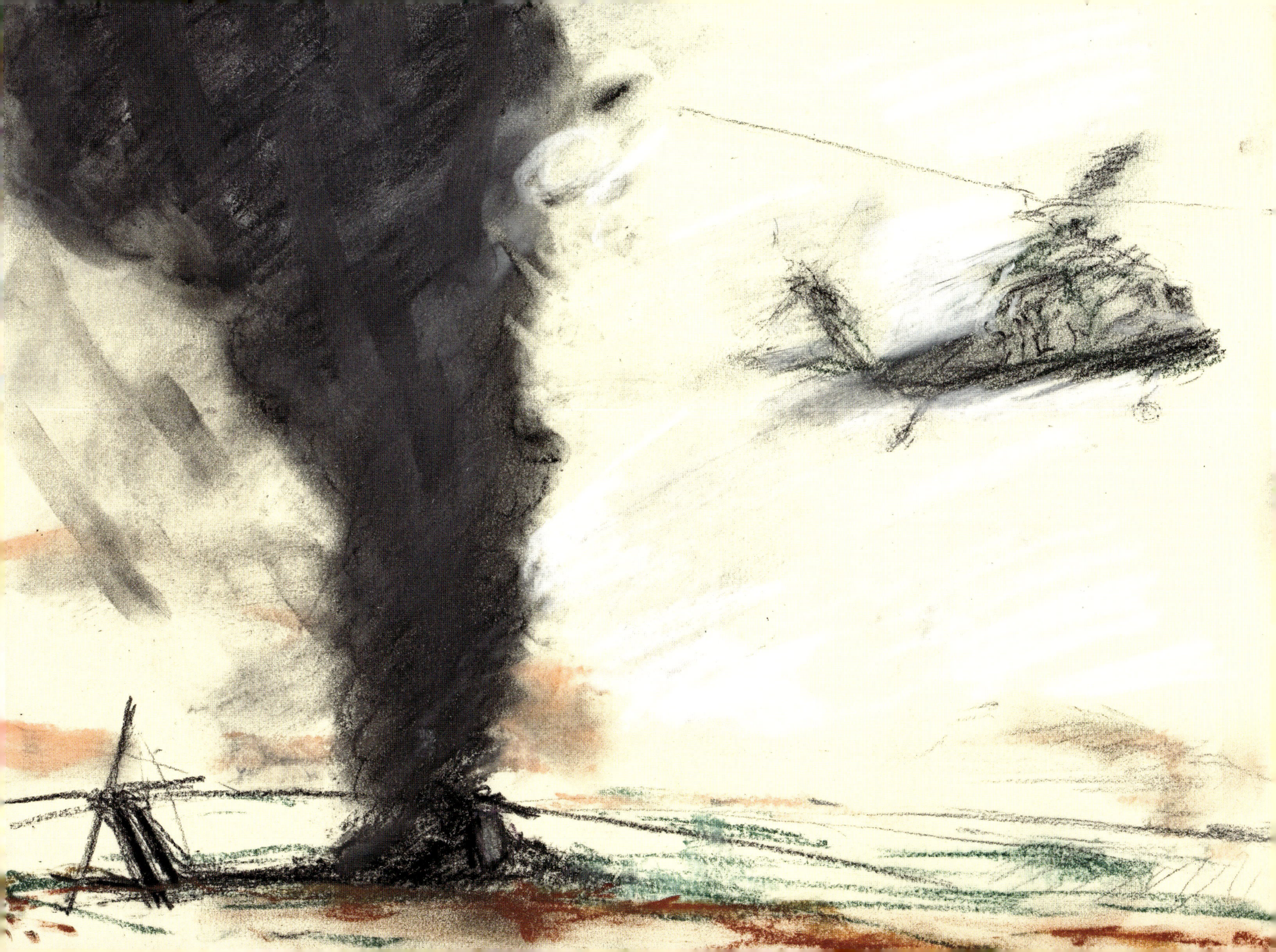

 Crash Landing V, 2004

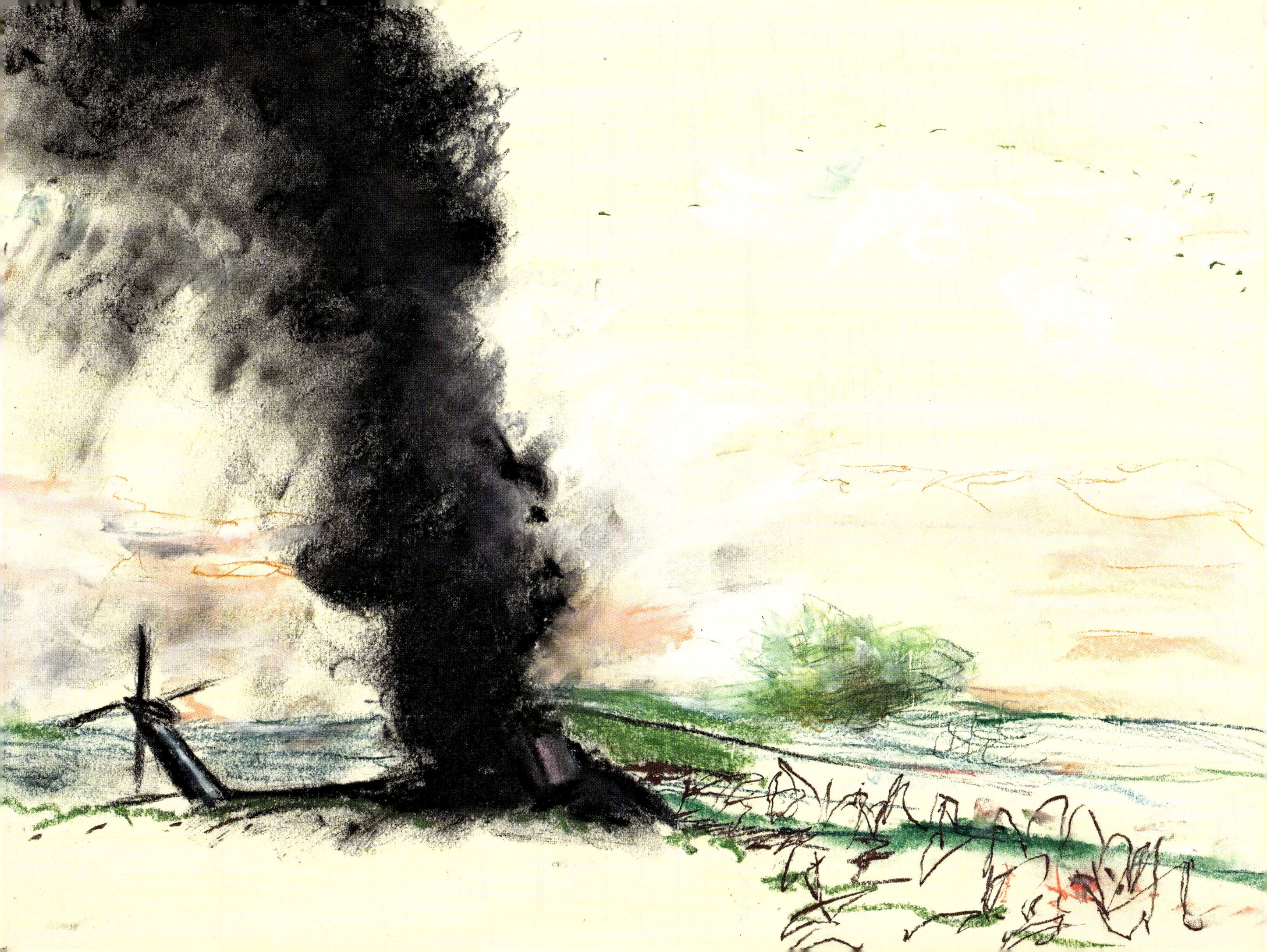

15 Crash Landing, 2004

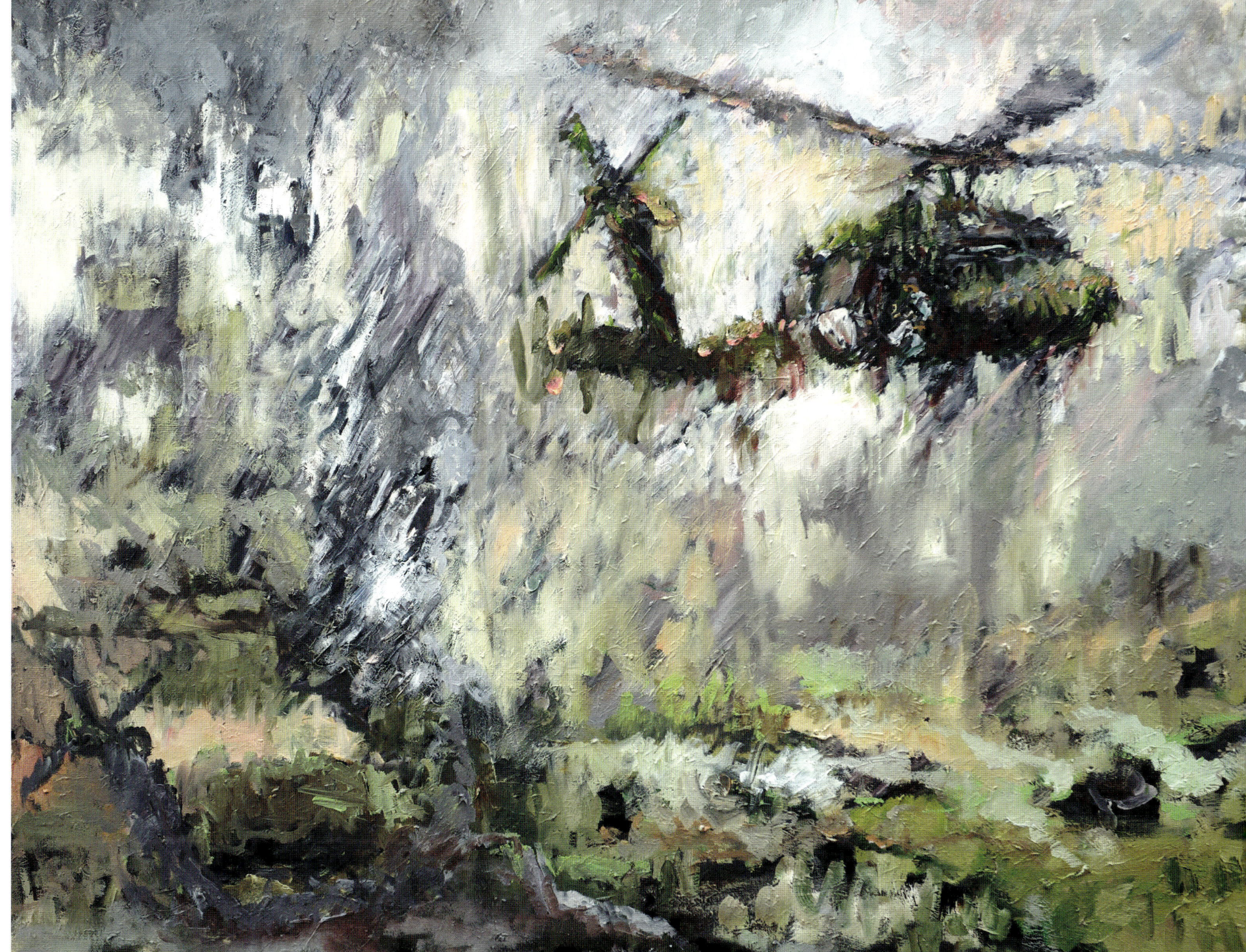

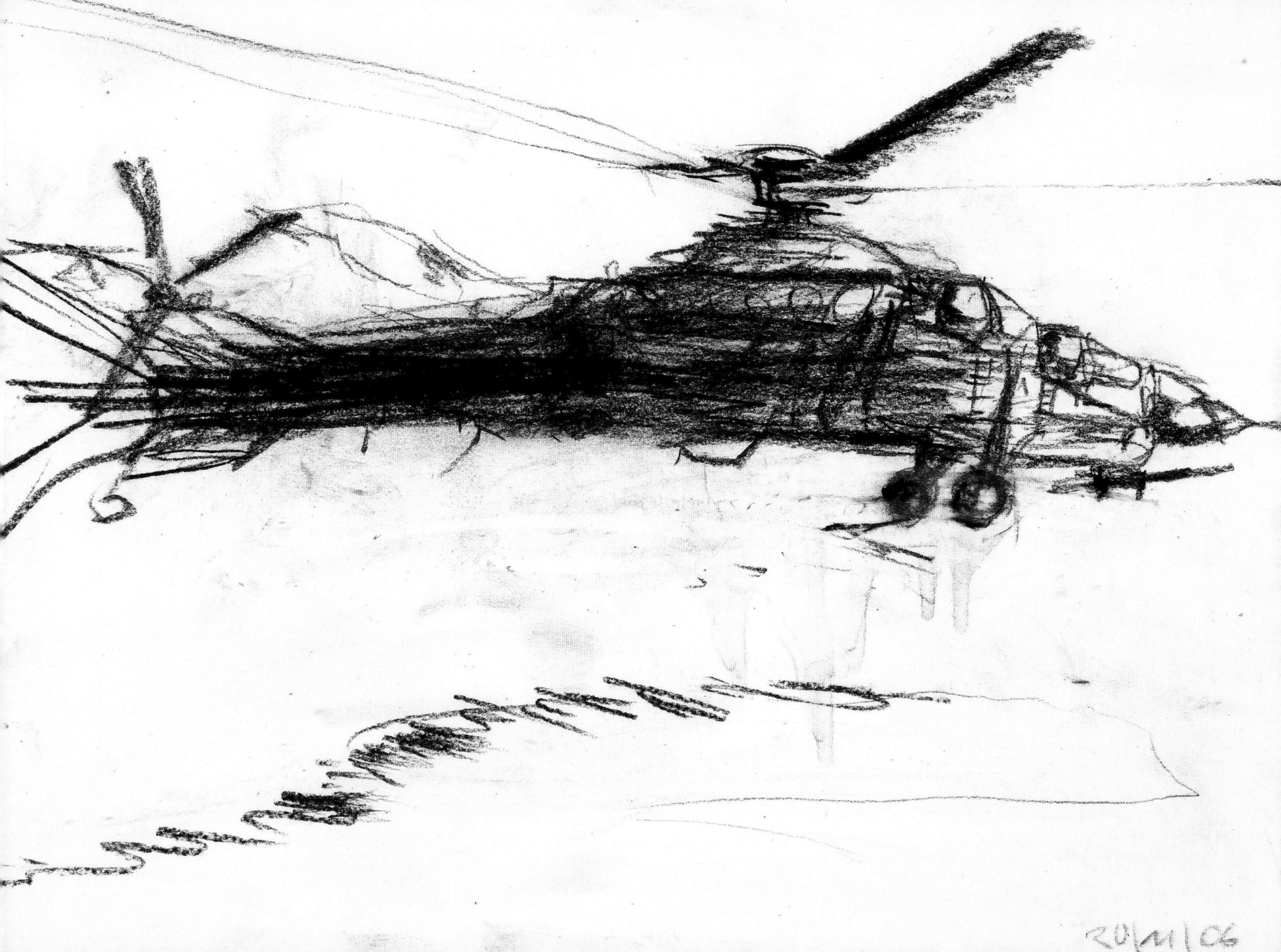
20|11|06

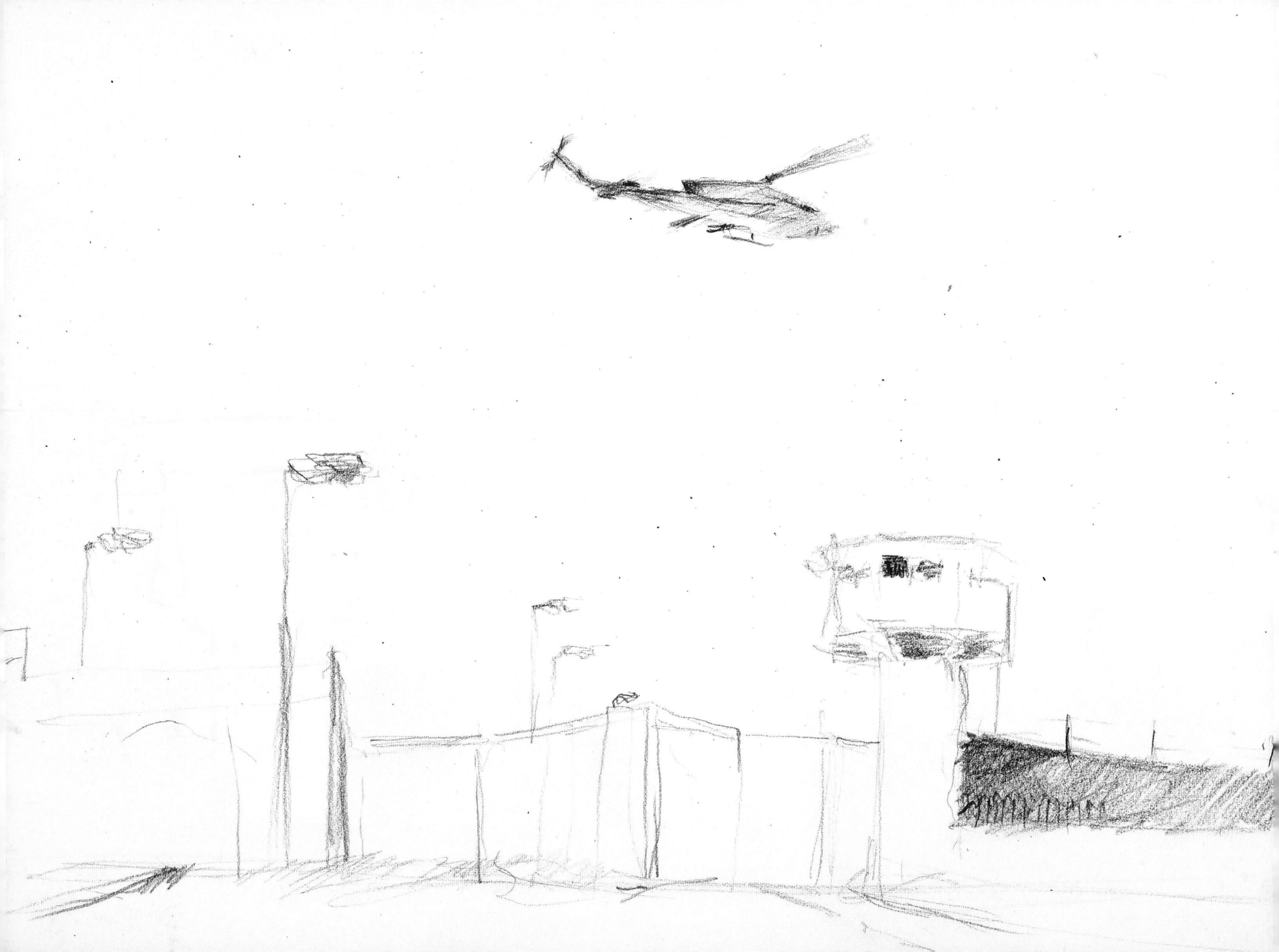

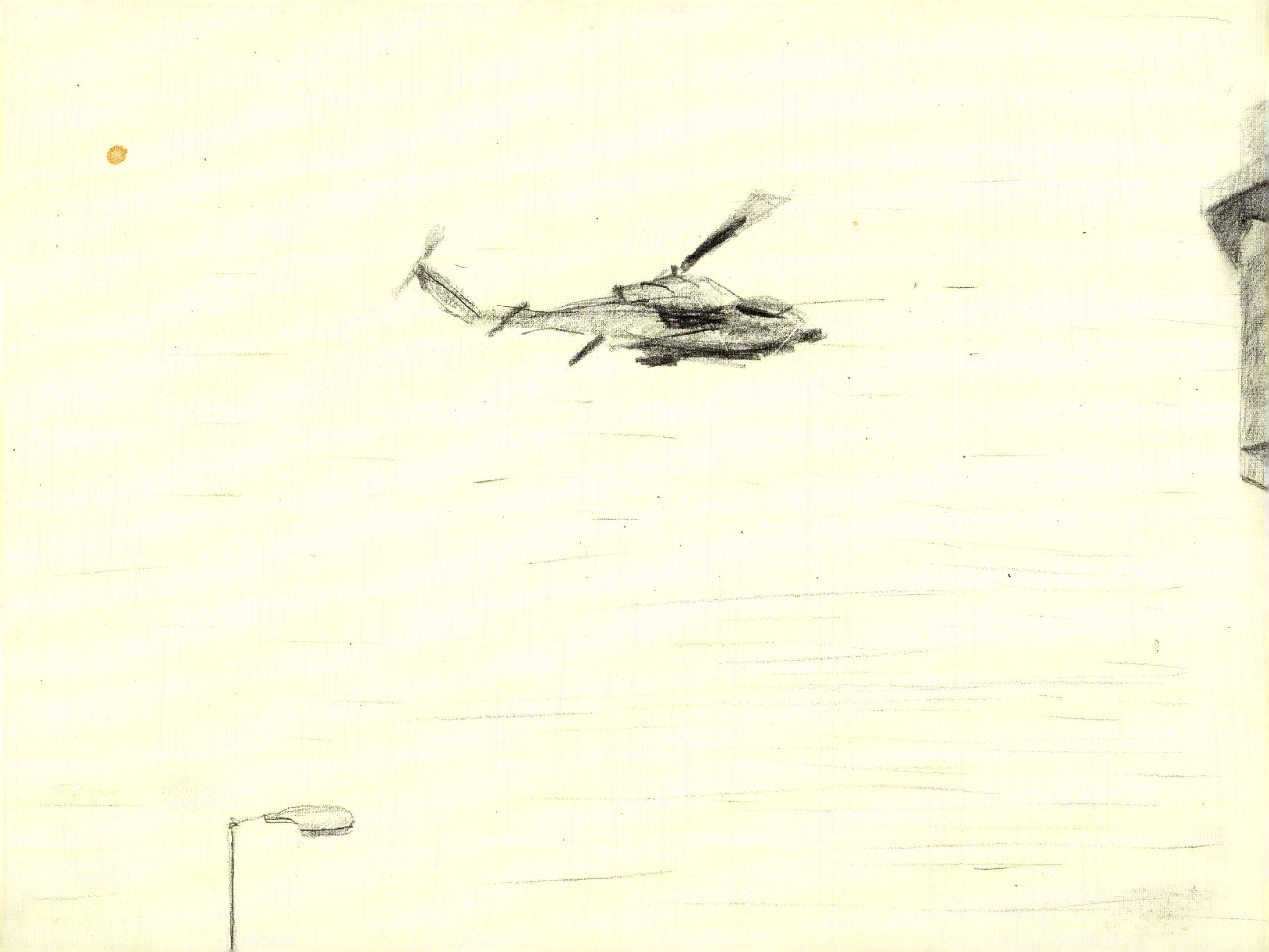

17 Surveillance II, 2003

18 Surveillance I, 2003

19 Surveillance III, 2003

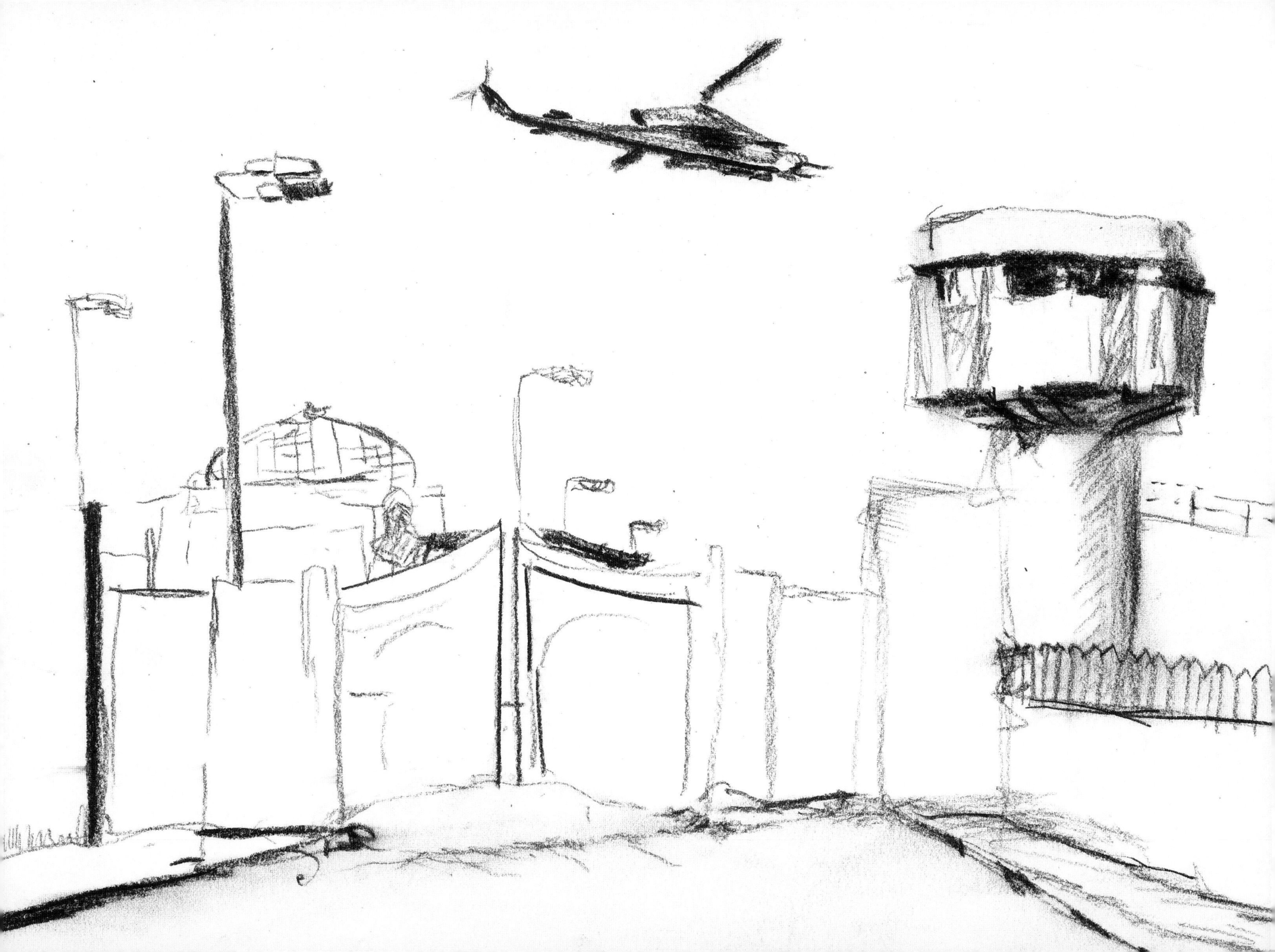

Dust, 2008

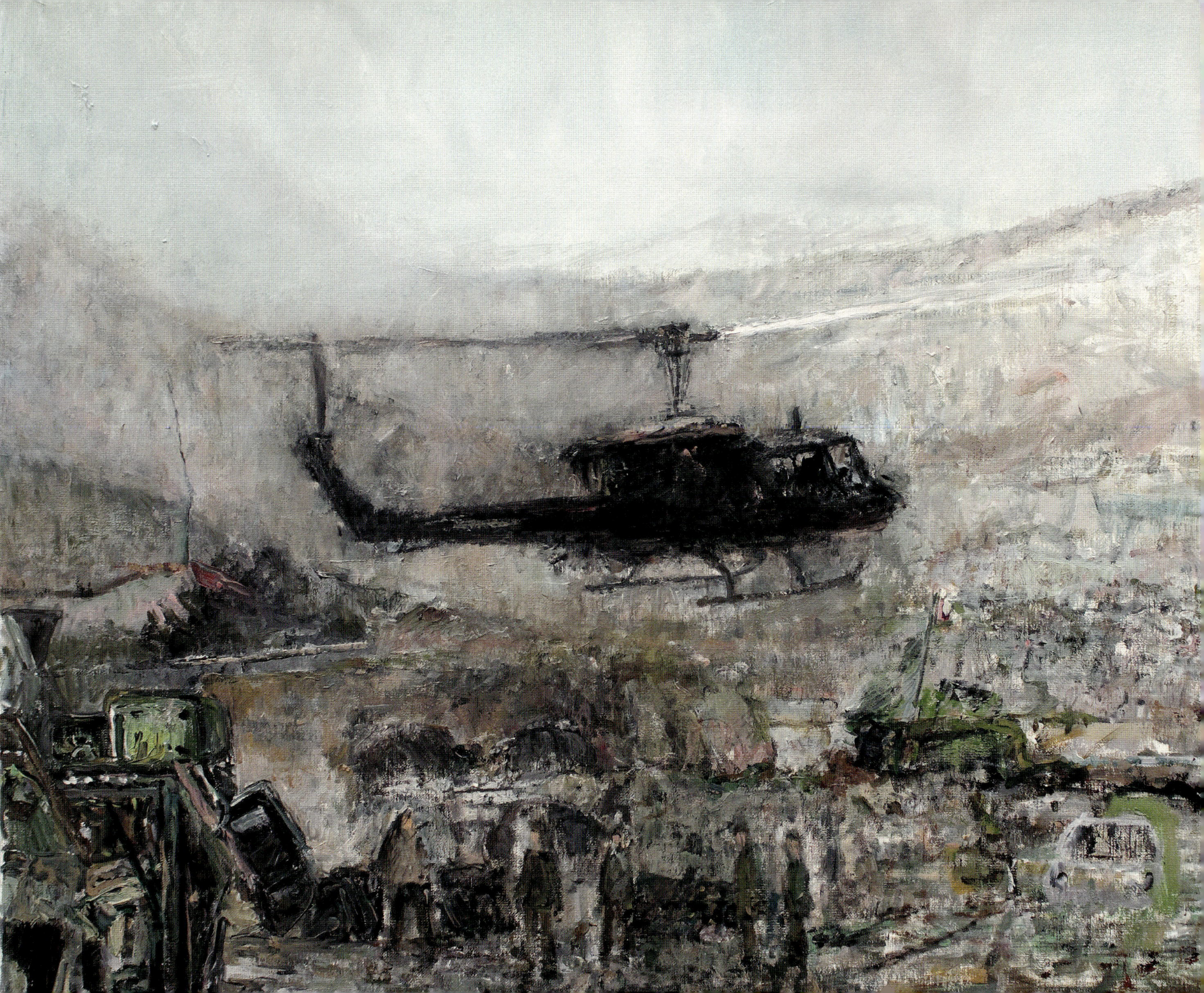

21 Soviet, 2012

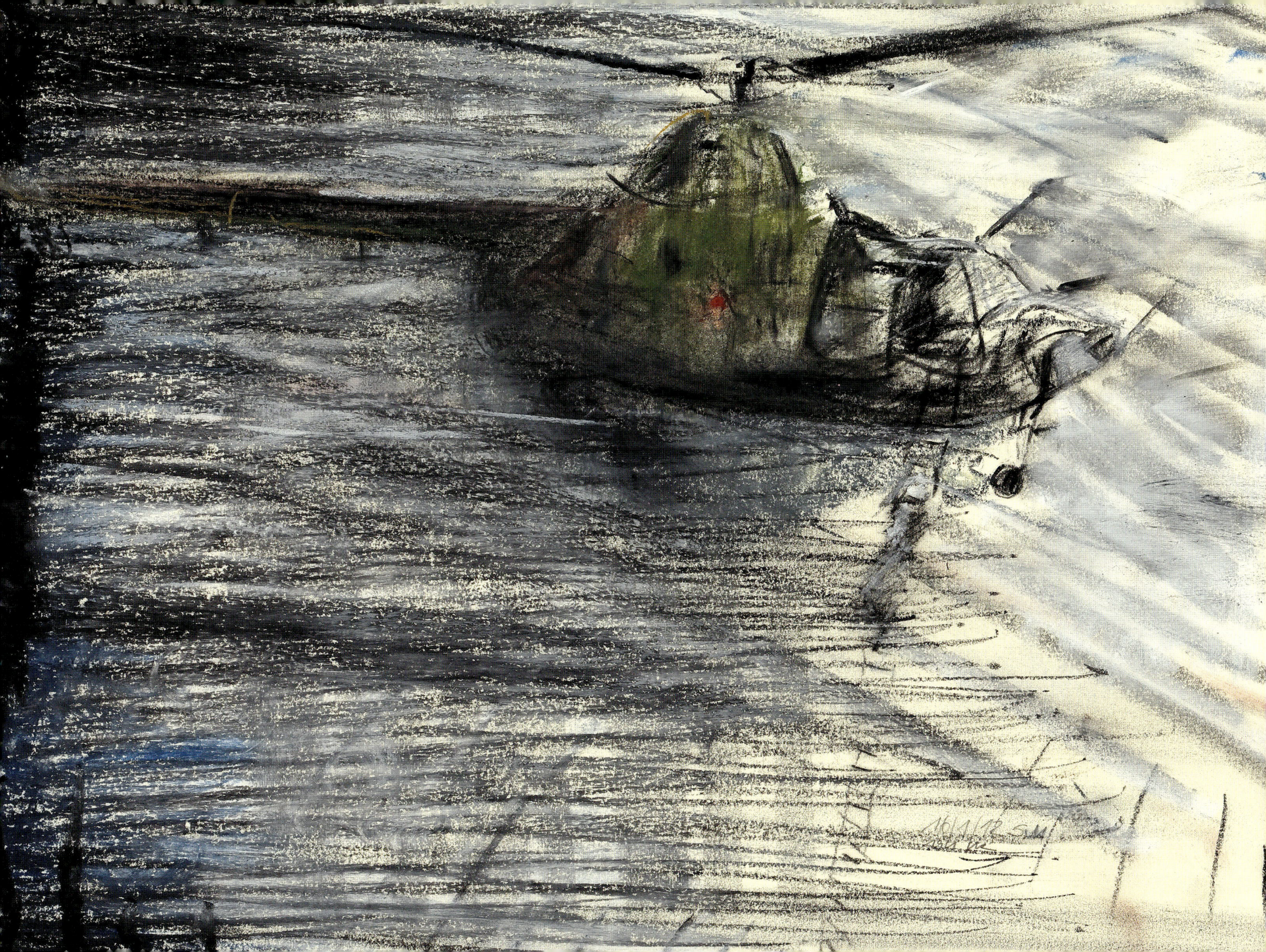

22 Siberia, 2012

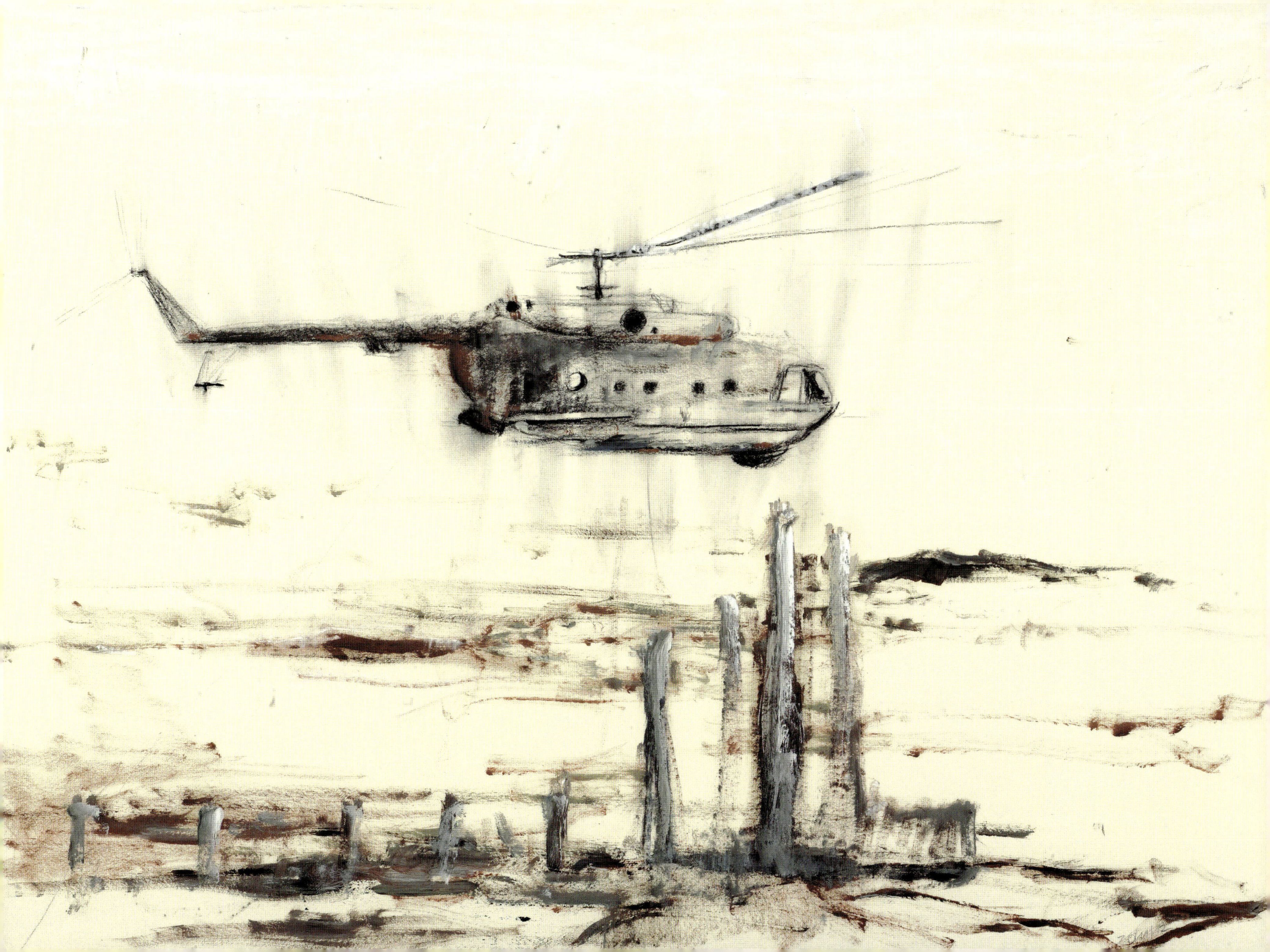

23 Aurora I, 2006

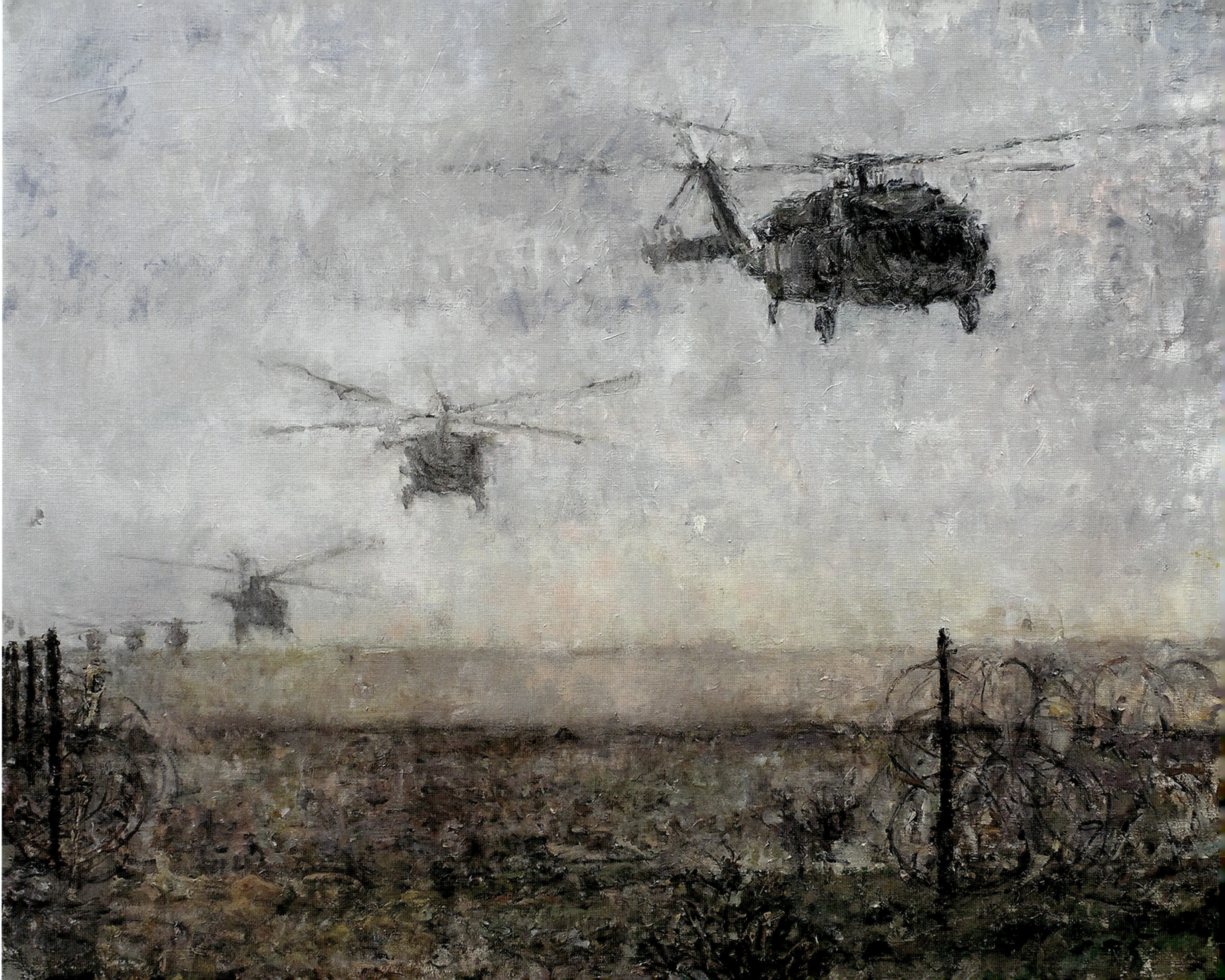

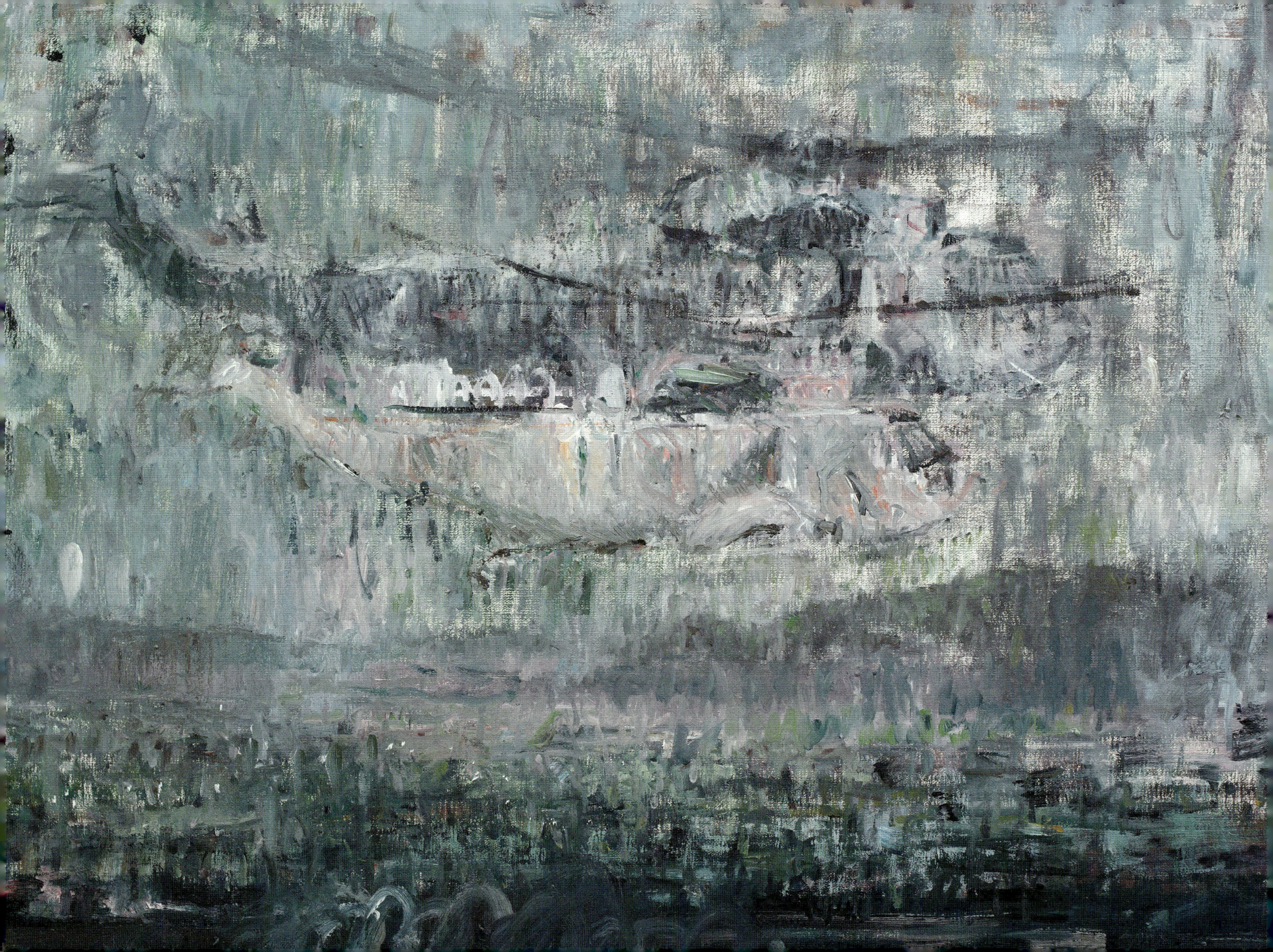

In the Morning

With dew the lawn is glistening; more nimbly now,
  Awake, the stream speeds onward; the beech inclines
    Her limber head and in the leaves a
      Rustle, a glitter begins; and round the

Grey cloud-banks there a flicker of reddish flames,
  Prophetic ones, flares up and in silence plays;
    Like breakers by the shore they billow
      Higher and higher, the ever-changing.

Now come, O come, and not too impatiently,
  You golden day, speed on to the peaks of heaven!
    For more familiar and more open,
      Glad one, my vision flies up towards you

While youthful in your beauty you gaze and have
  Not grown too glorious, dazzling and proud for me;
    Speed as you will, I'd say, if only
      I could go with you, divinely ranging!

But at my happy arrogance now you smile,
  That would be like you; rather, then, rambler, bless
    My mortal acts, and this day also,
      Kindly one, brighten my quiet pathway.

Des Morgens

Vom Thaue glänzt der Rasen; beweglicher
  Eilt schon die wache Quelle; die Buche neigt
    Ihr schwankes Haupt und im Geblätter
      Rauscht es und schimmert; und um die grauen

Gewölke streifen röthliche flammen dort,
  Verkündende, sie wallen geräuschlos auf;
    Wie Fluthen am Gestade, woogen
      Höher und höher die Wandelbaren.

Komm nun, o komm, und eile mir nicht zu schnell,
  Du goldner Tag, zum Gipfel des Himmels fort!
    Denn offner fliegt, vertrauter dir mein
      Auge, du Freudiger! zu, solang du

In deiner Schöne jugendlich blikst und noch
  Zu herrlich nicht, zu stolz mir geworden bist;
    Du möchtest immer eilen, könnt ich,
      Göttlicher Wandrer, mit dir! – doch lächelst

Des frohen übermüthigen du, daß er
  Dir gleichen möchte; seegne mir lieber dann
    Mein sterblich Thun und heitre wieder
      Gütiger! heute den stillen Pfad mir.

Friedrich Hölderlin, 1799

Evening Fantasy

At peace the ploughman sits in the shade outside
His cottage; smoke curls up from his modest hearth.
A traveller hears the bell for vespers
Welcome him in to a quiet village.

Now too the boatmen make for the harbour pool,
In distant towns the market's gay noise and throng
Subside; a glittering meal awaits the
Friends in the garden's most hidden arbour.

But where shall I go? Does not a mortal live
By work and wages? Balancing toil with rest
All makes him glad. Must I alone then
Find no relief from the thorn that goads me?

A springtime buds high up in the evening sky,
There countless roses bloom, and the golden world
Seems calm, fulfilled; O there now take me,
Crimson-edged clouds, and up there at last let

My love and sorrow melt into light and air! –
As if that foolish plea had dispersed it, though,
The spell breaks; darkness falls, and lonely
Under the heavens I stand as always. –

Now you come, gentle sleep! For the heart demands
Too much; but youth at last, you the dreamy, wild,
Unquiet, will burn out, and leave me
All my late years for serene contentment.

Abendphantasie

Vor seiner Hütte ruhig im Schatten sizt
Der Pflüger, dem Genügsamen raucht sein Heerd.
Gastfreundlich tönt dem Wanderer im
Friedlichen Dorfe die Abendgloke.

Wohl kehren itzt die Schiffer zum Hafen auch,
In fernen Städten, fröhlich verrauscht des Markts
Geschäfft' ger Lärm; in stiller Laube
Glänzt das gesellige Mahl den Freunden.

Wohin denn ich? Es leben die Sterblichen
Von Lohn und Arbeit; wechselnd in Müh' und Ruh'
Ist alles freudig; warum schläft denn
Nimmer nur mir in der Brust der Stachel?

Am Abendhimmel blühet ein Frühling auf;
Unzählig blühn die Rosen und ruhig scheint
Die goldne Welt; o dorthin nimmt mich,
Purpurne Wolken! und möge droben

In Licht und Luft zerrinnen mir Lieb' und Laid! –
Doch, wie verscheucht von thöriger Bitte, flieht
Der Zauber; dunkel wirds und einsam
Unter dem Himmel, wie immer, bin ich –

Komm du nun, sanfter Schlummer! zu viel begehrt
Das Herz; doch endlich, Jugend! verglühst du ja,
Du ruhelose, träumerische!
Friedlich und heiter ist dann das Alter.

Friedrich Hölderlin, 1799

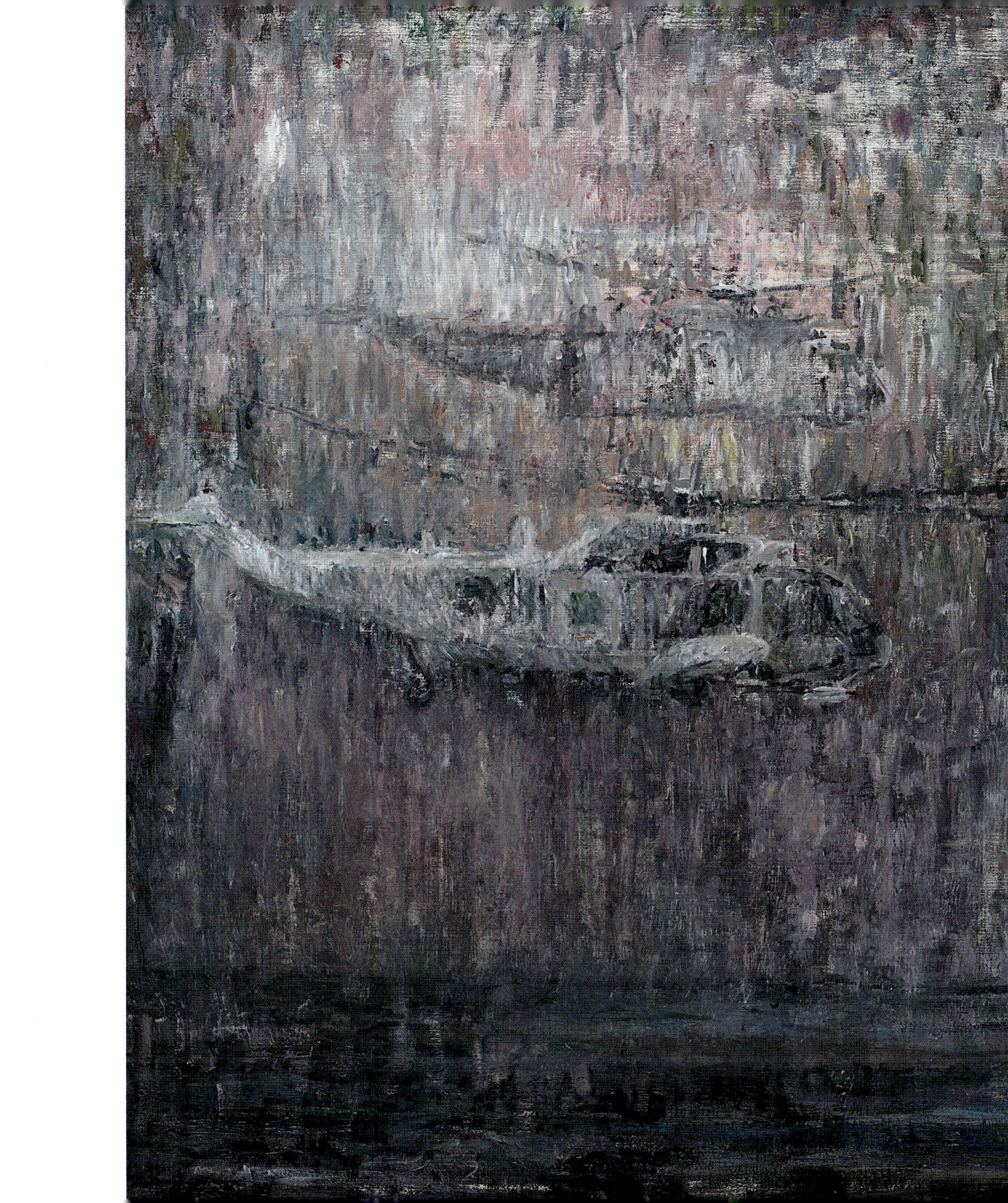

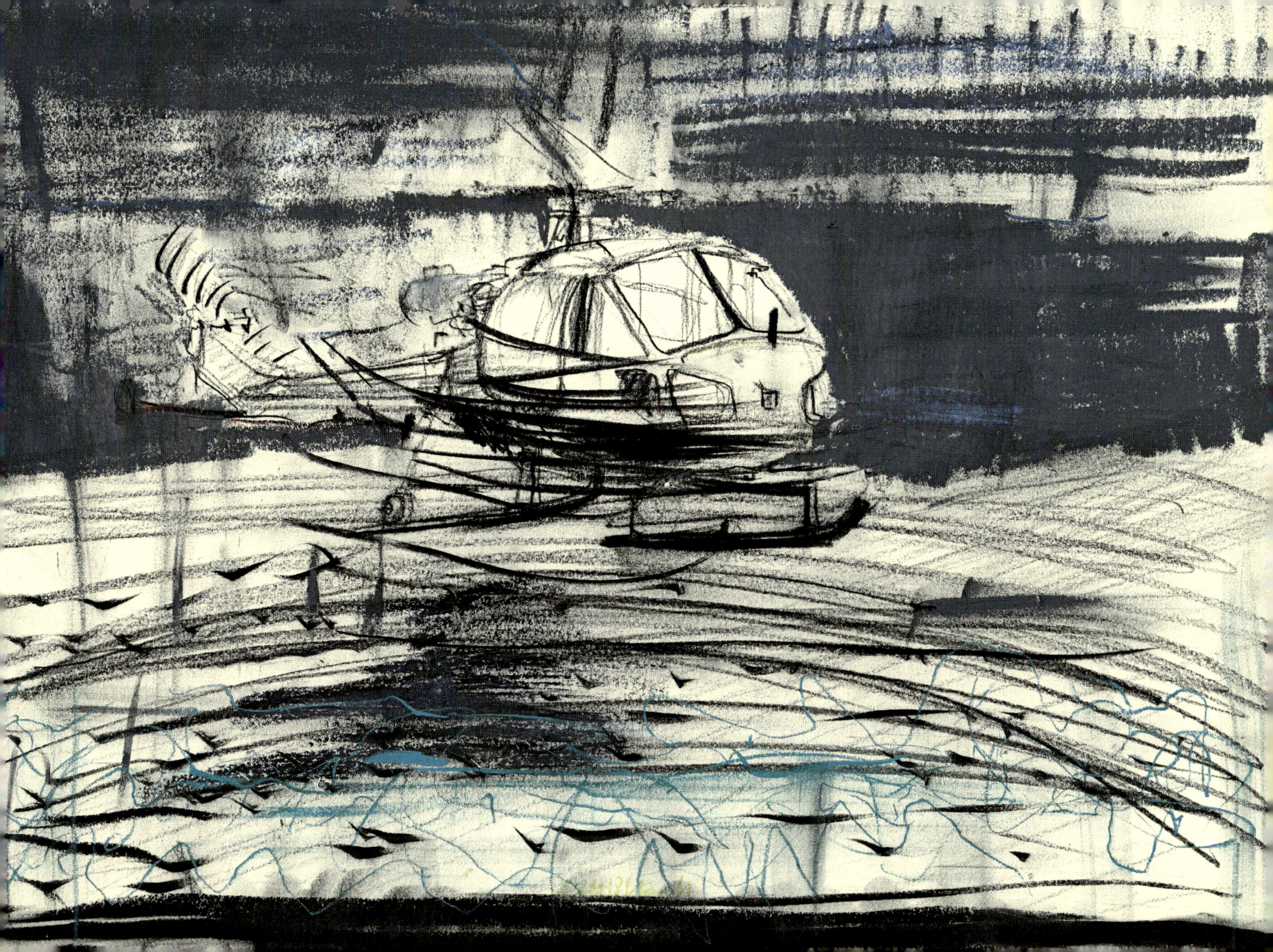

27 Blue, 2010

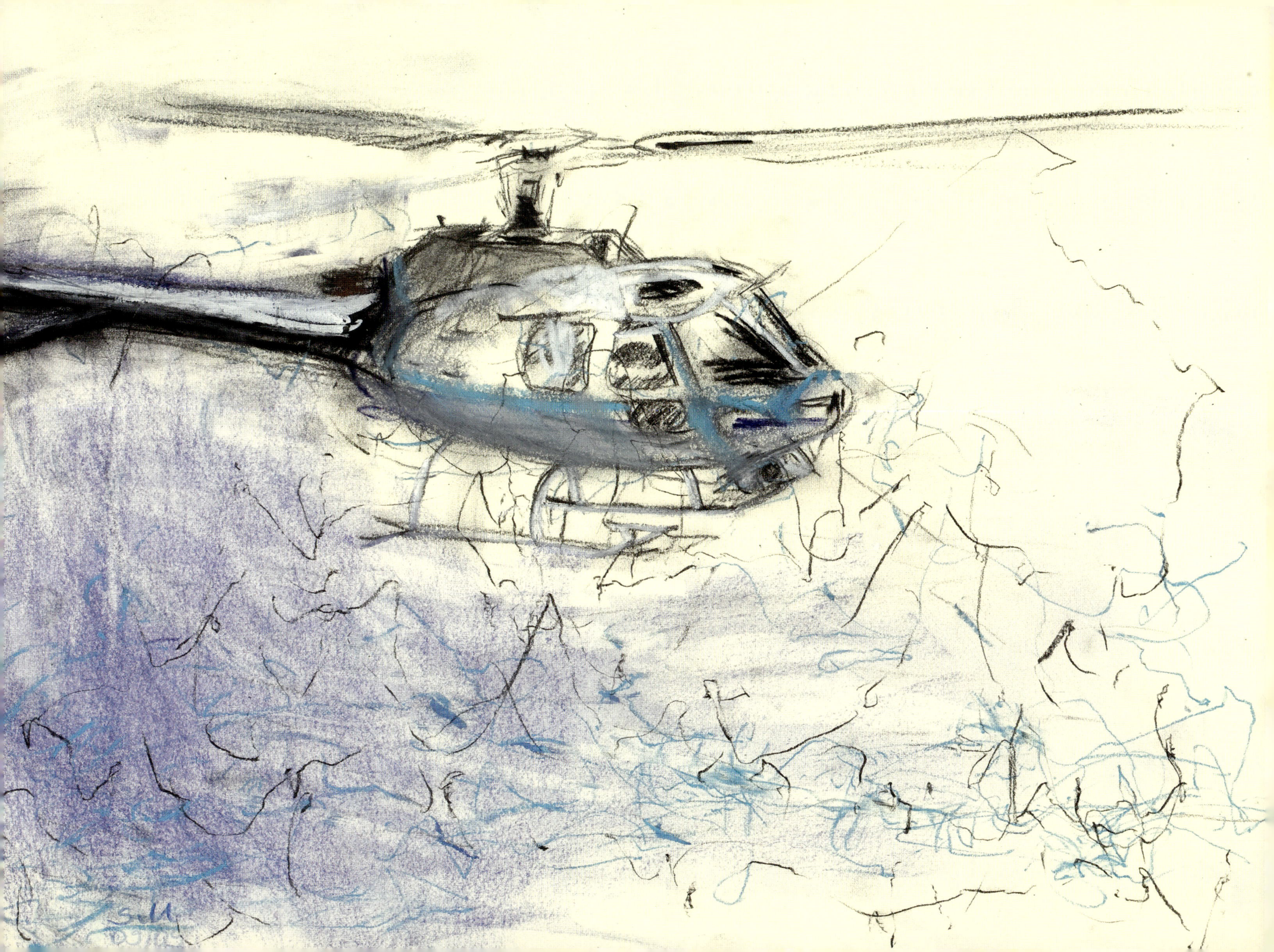

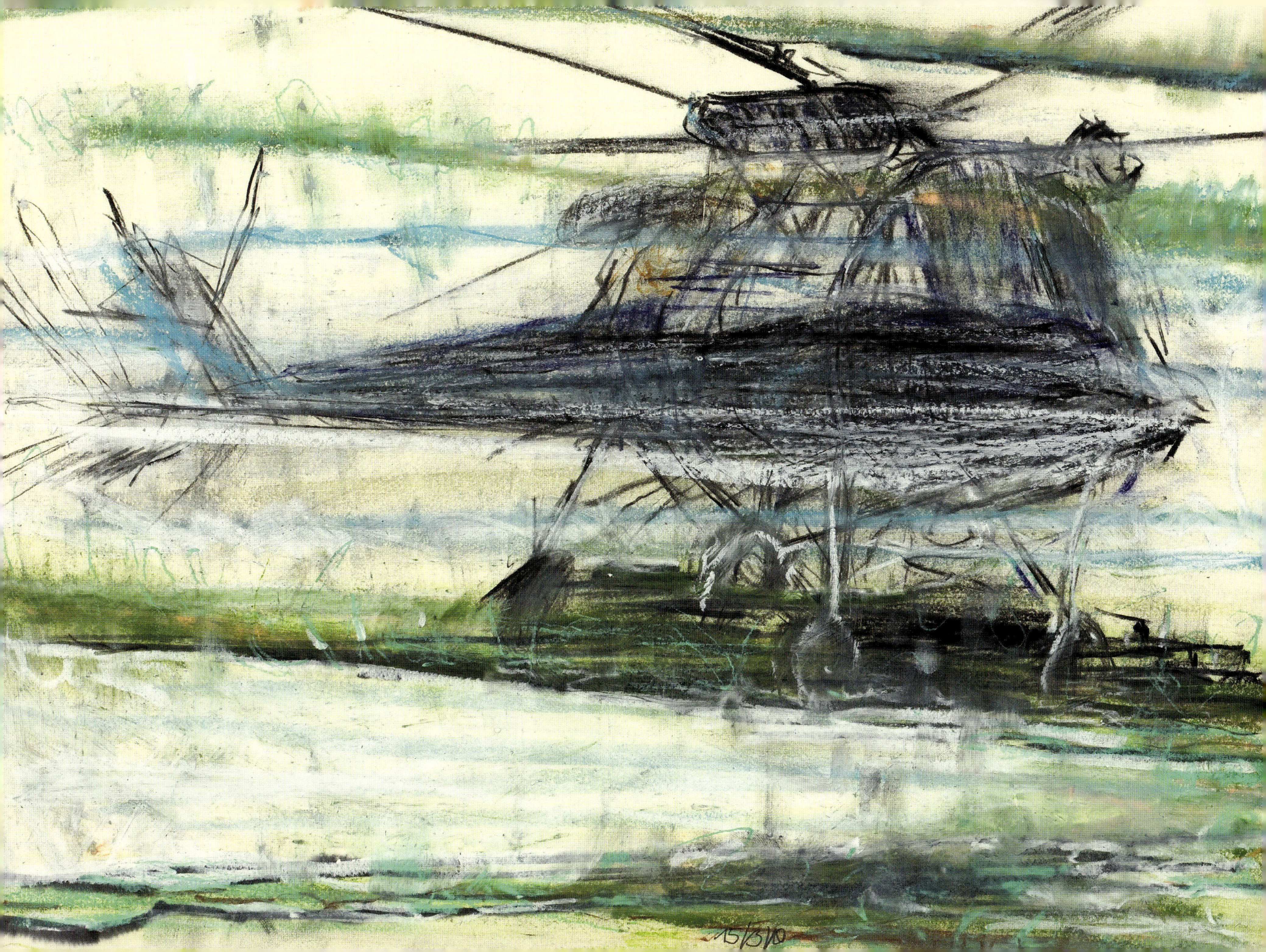
15/3/10

29 Pink, 2010

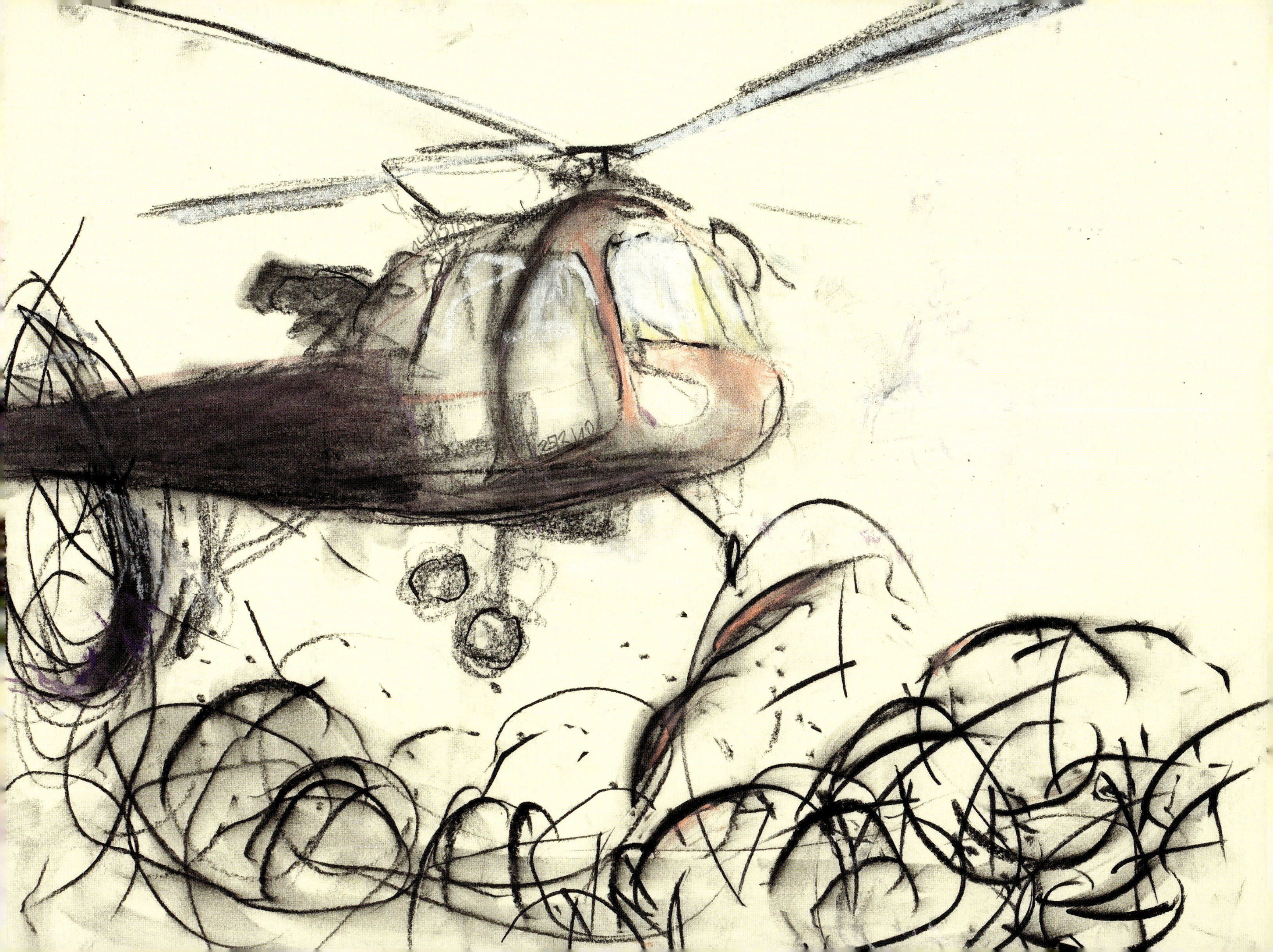

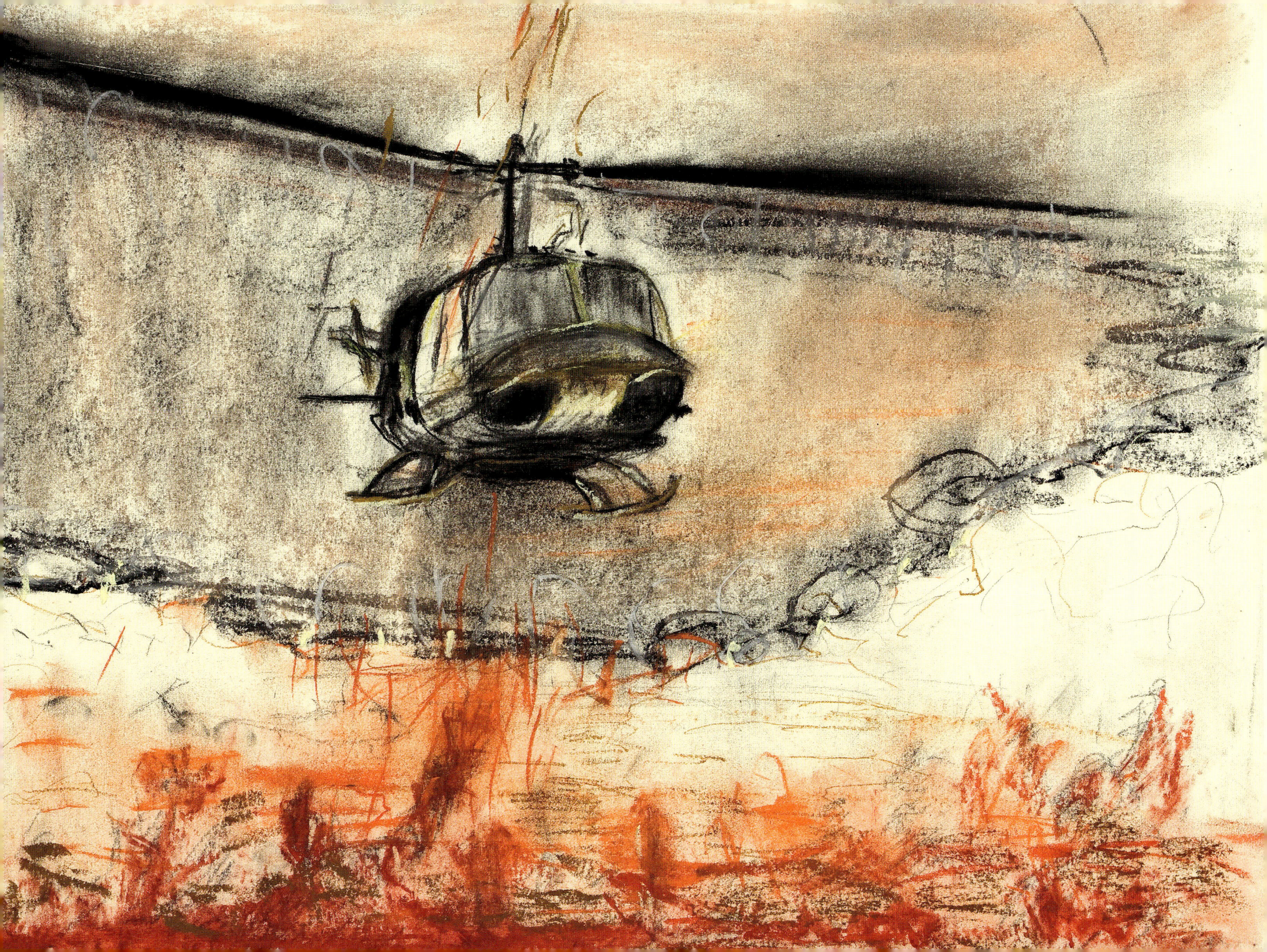

31 Mother, 2010

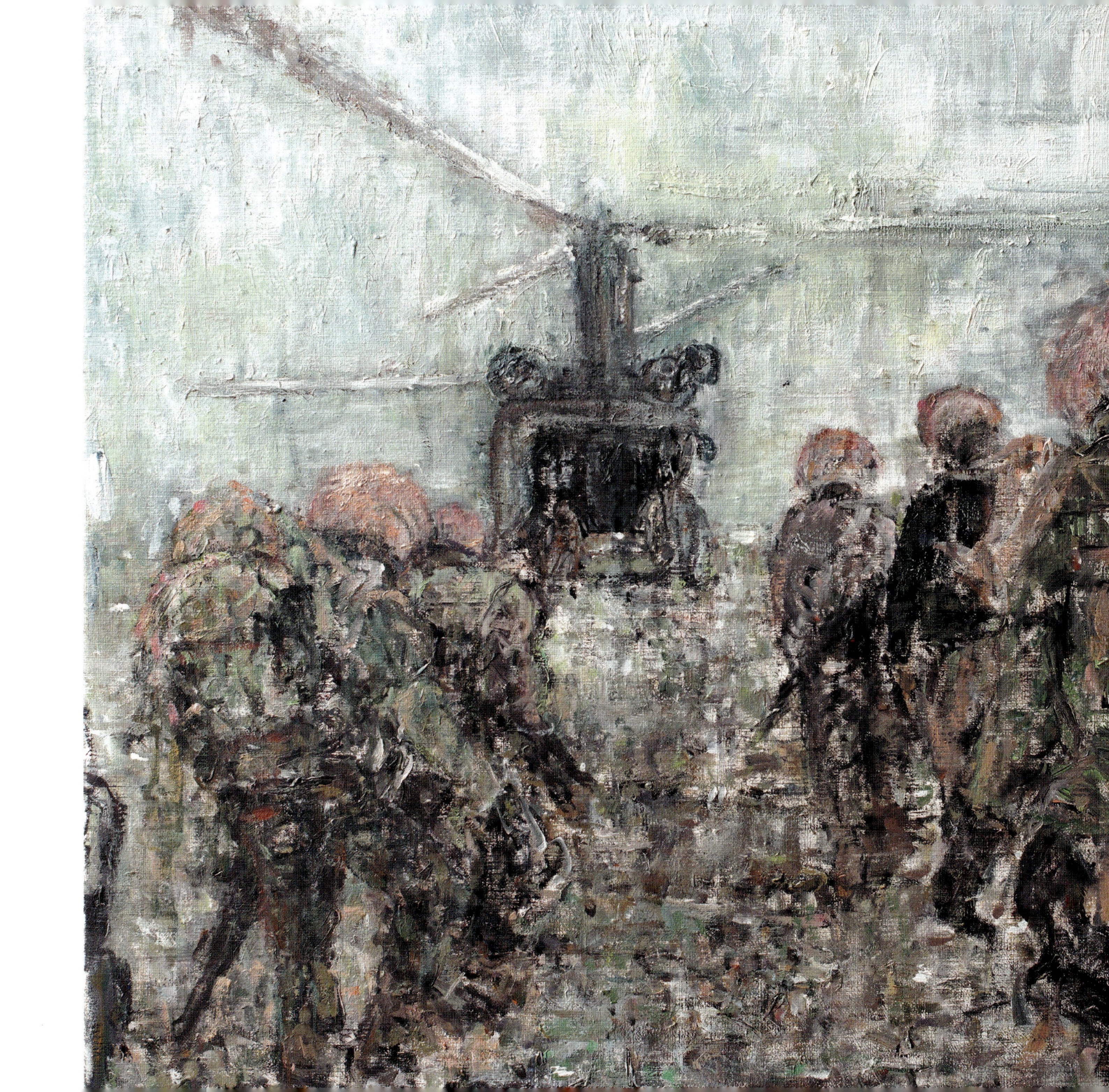

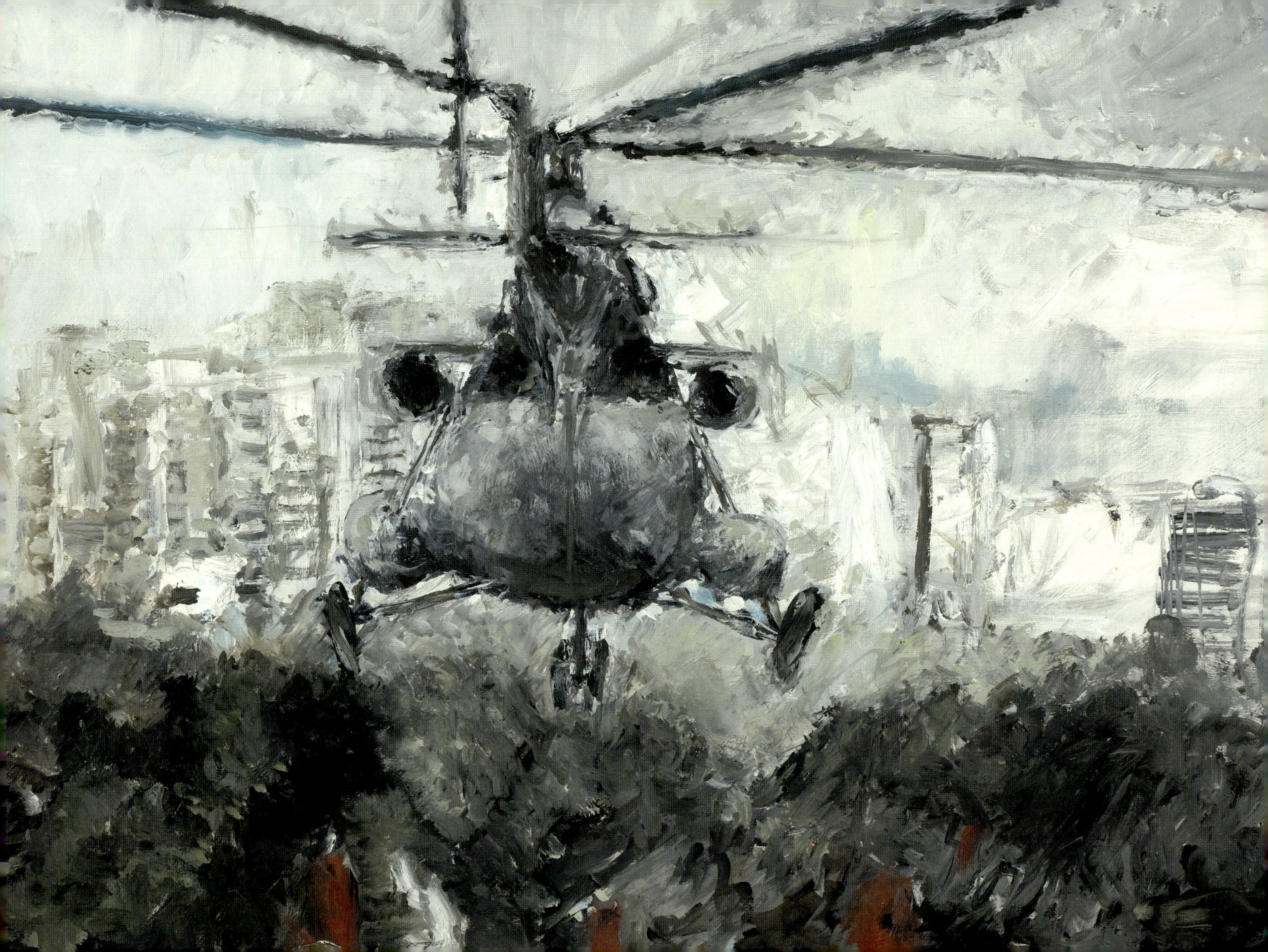

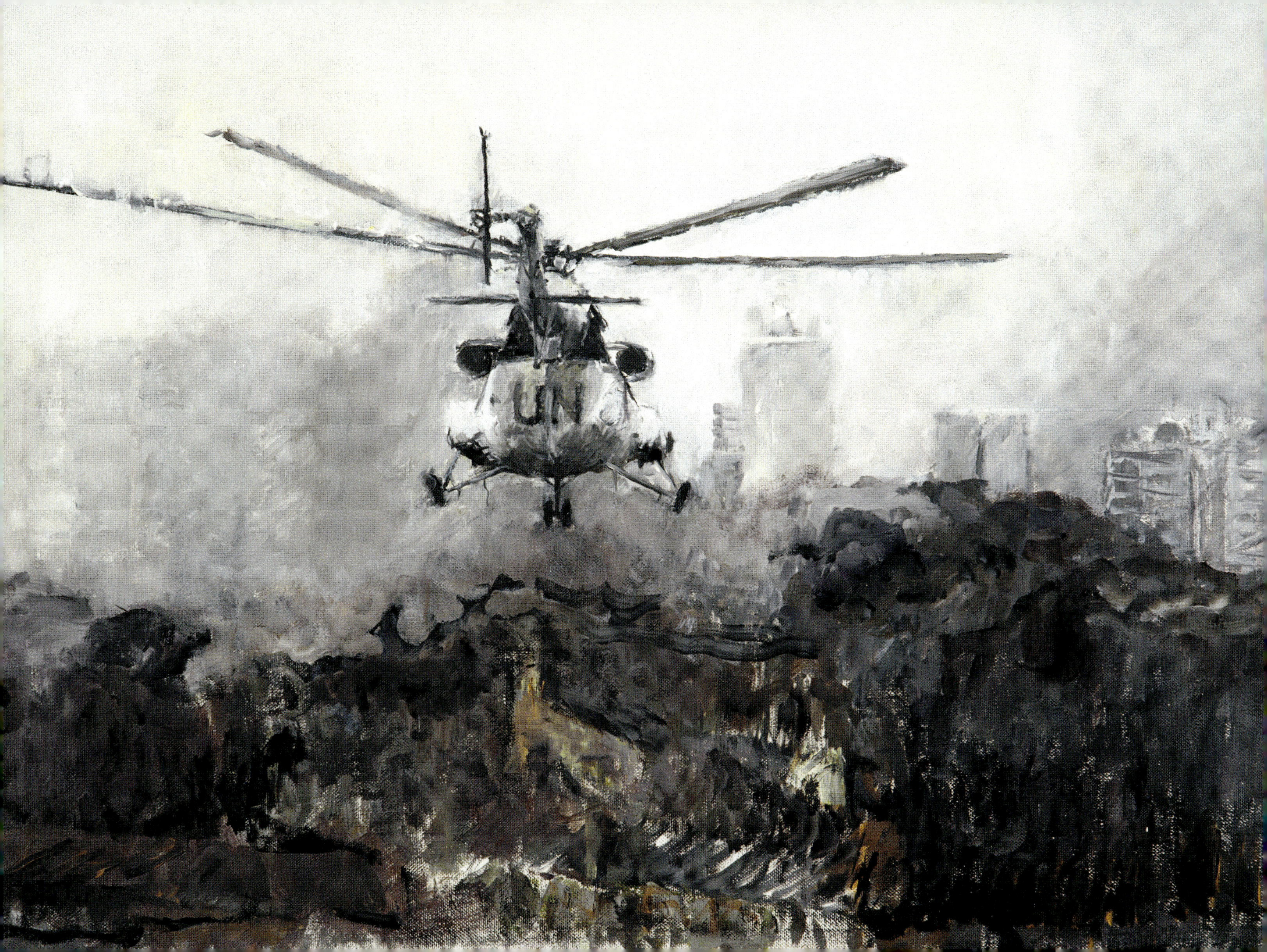
UN

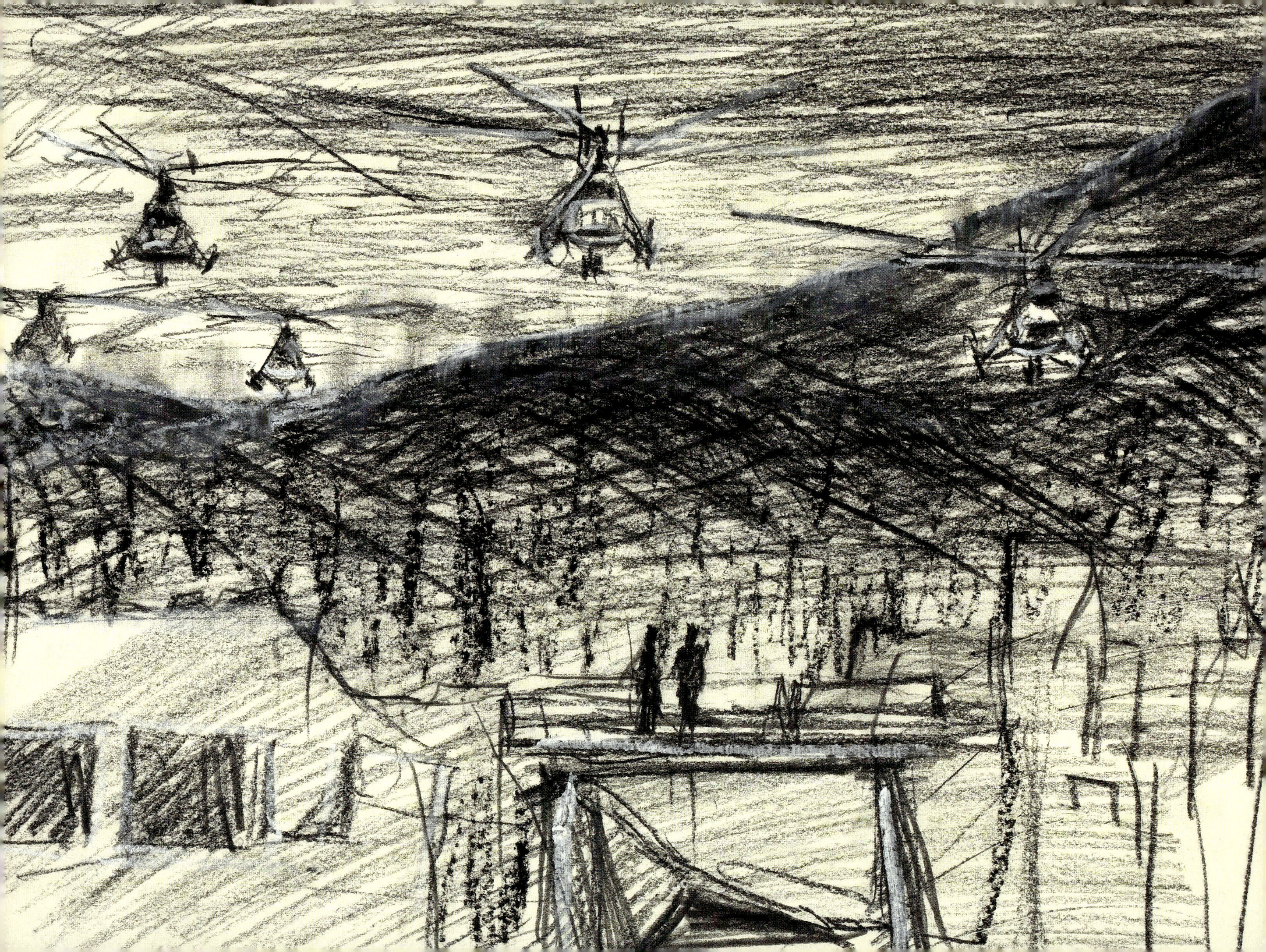

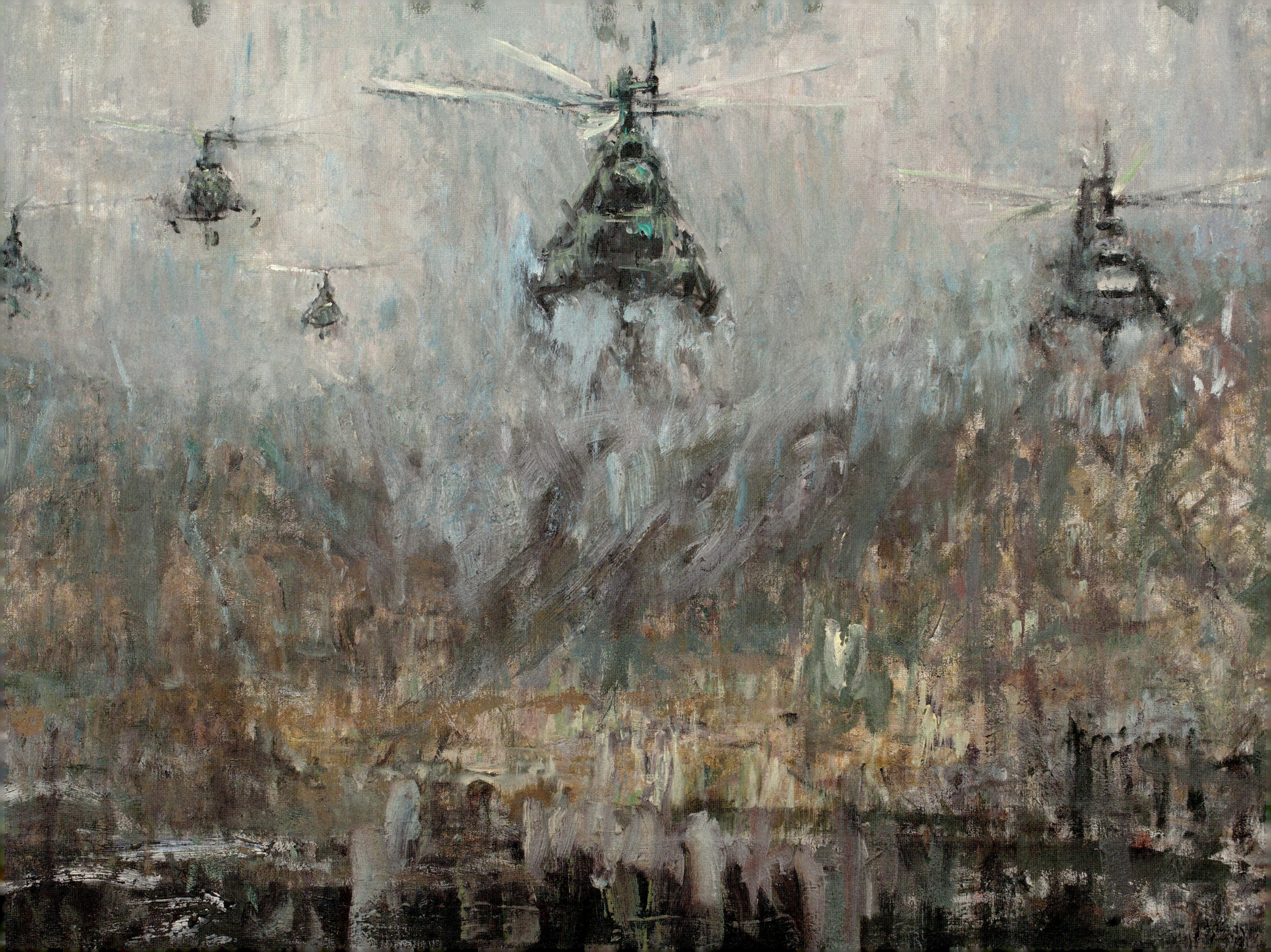

32 Macbeth, 2005

33 Kinshasa, 2004

34 Parade (Sketch), 2006

35 Parade II, 2010

36 Parade I, 2007

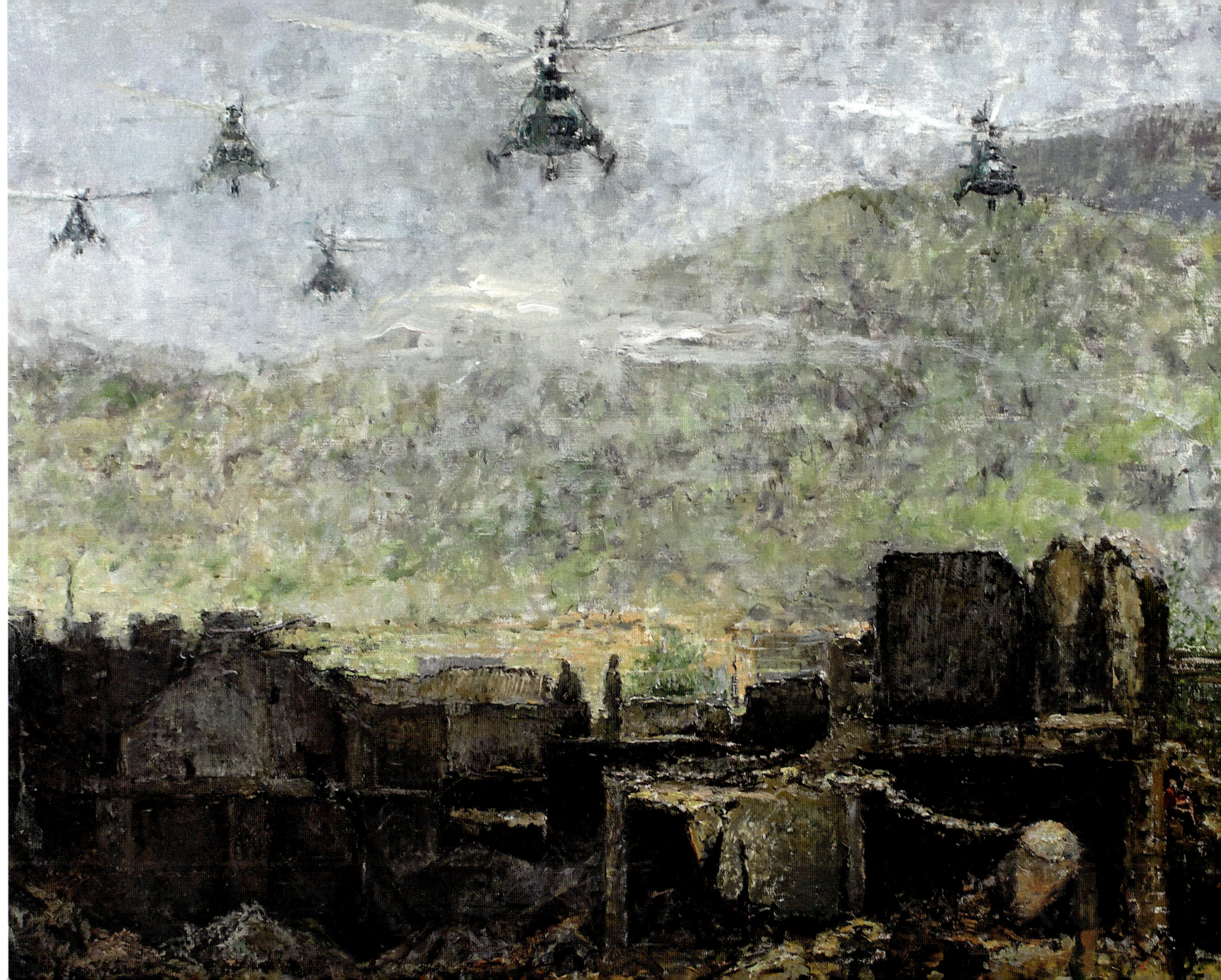

37 Attack, 2009

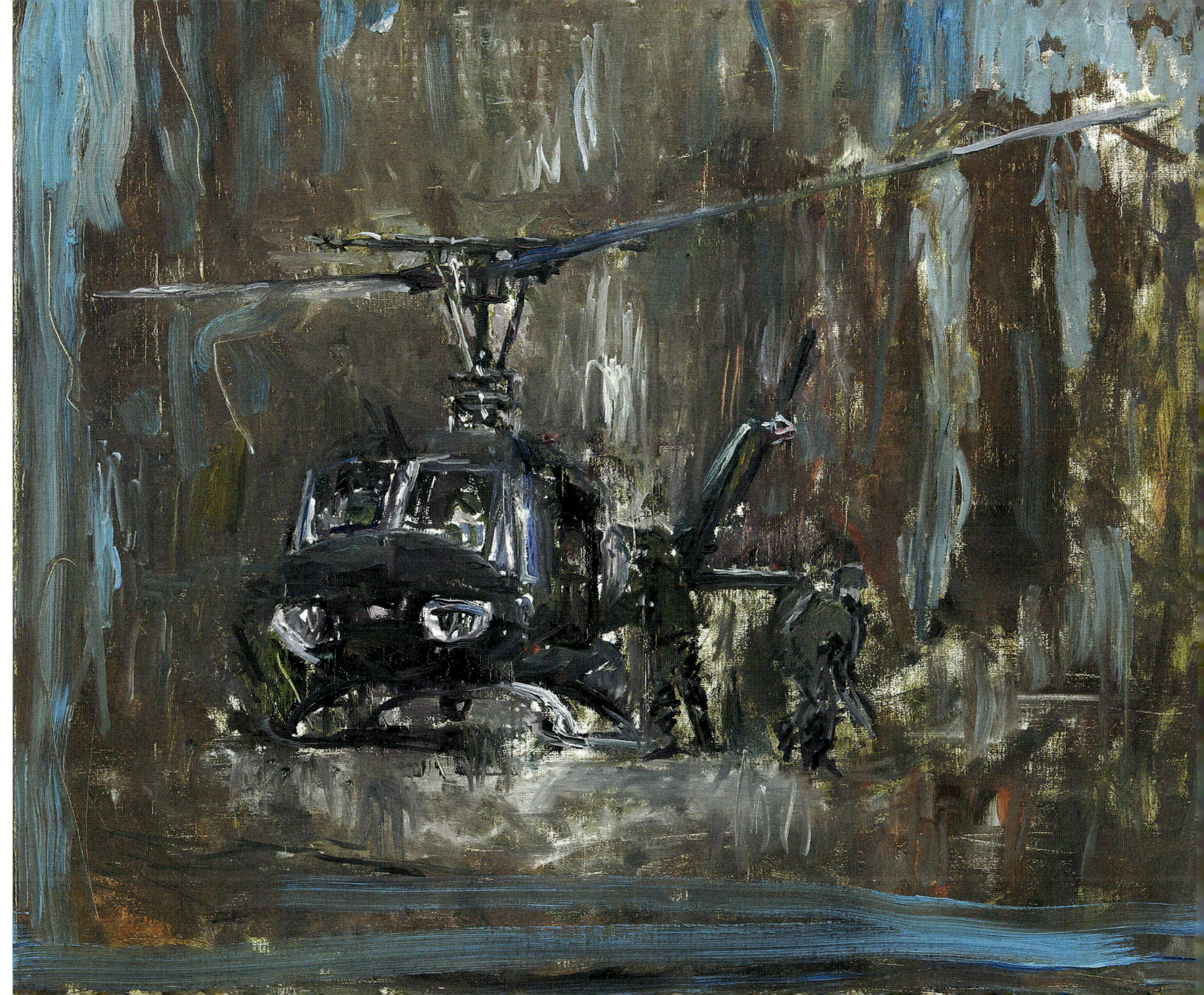

Jungle, 2010

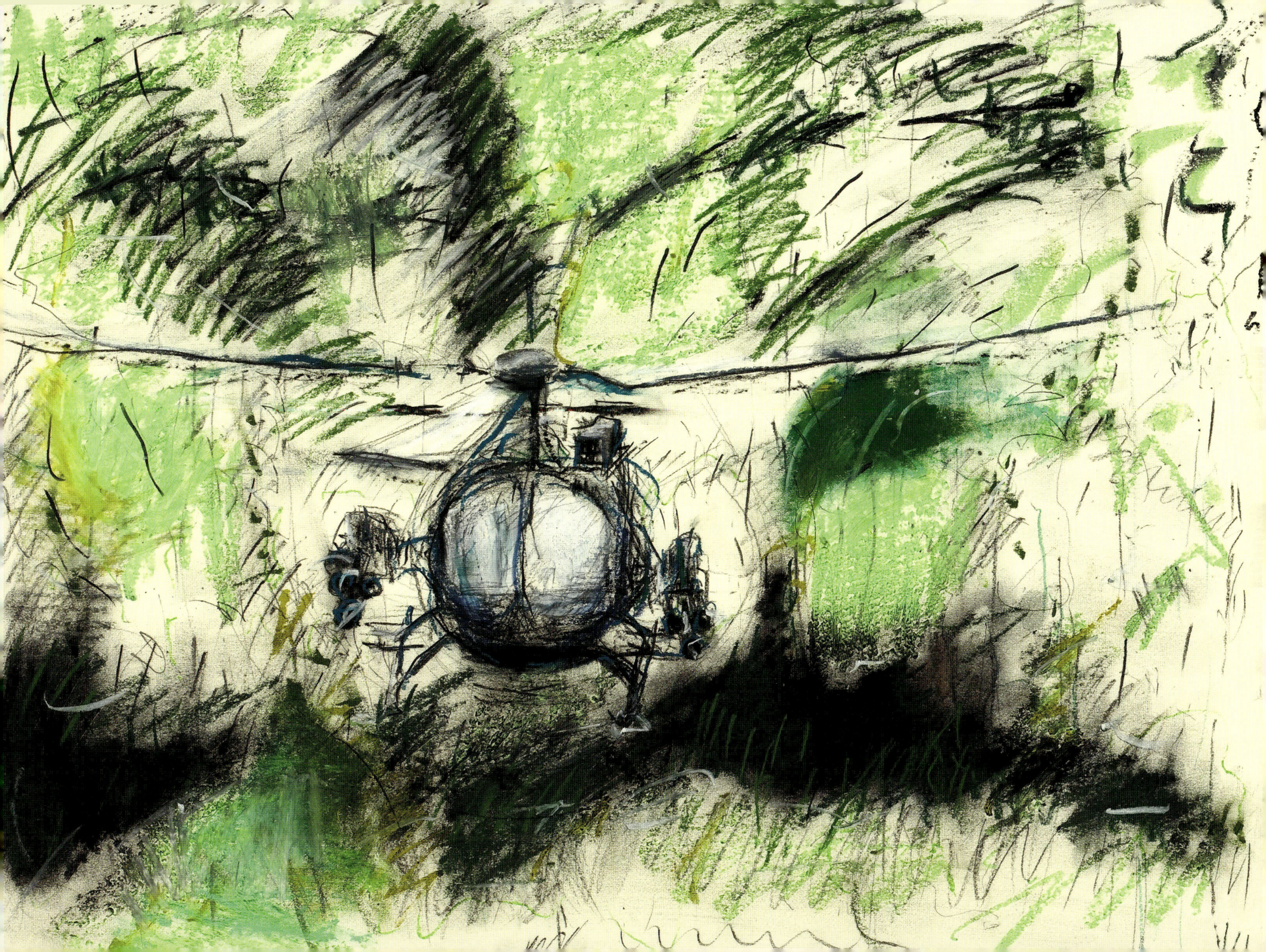

39 Deadline, 2004

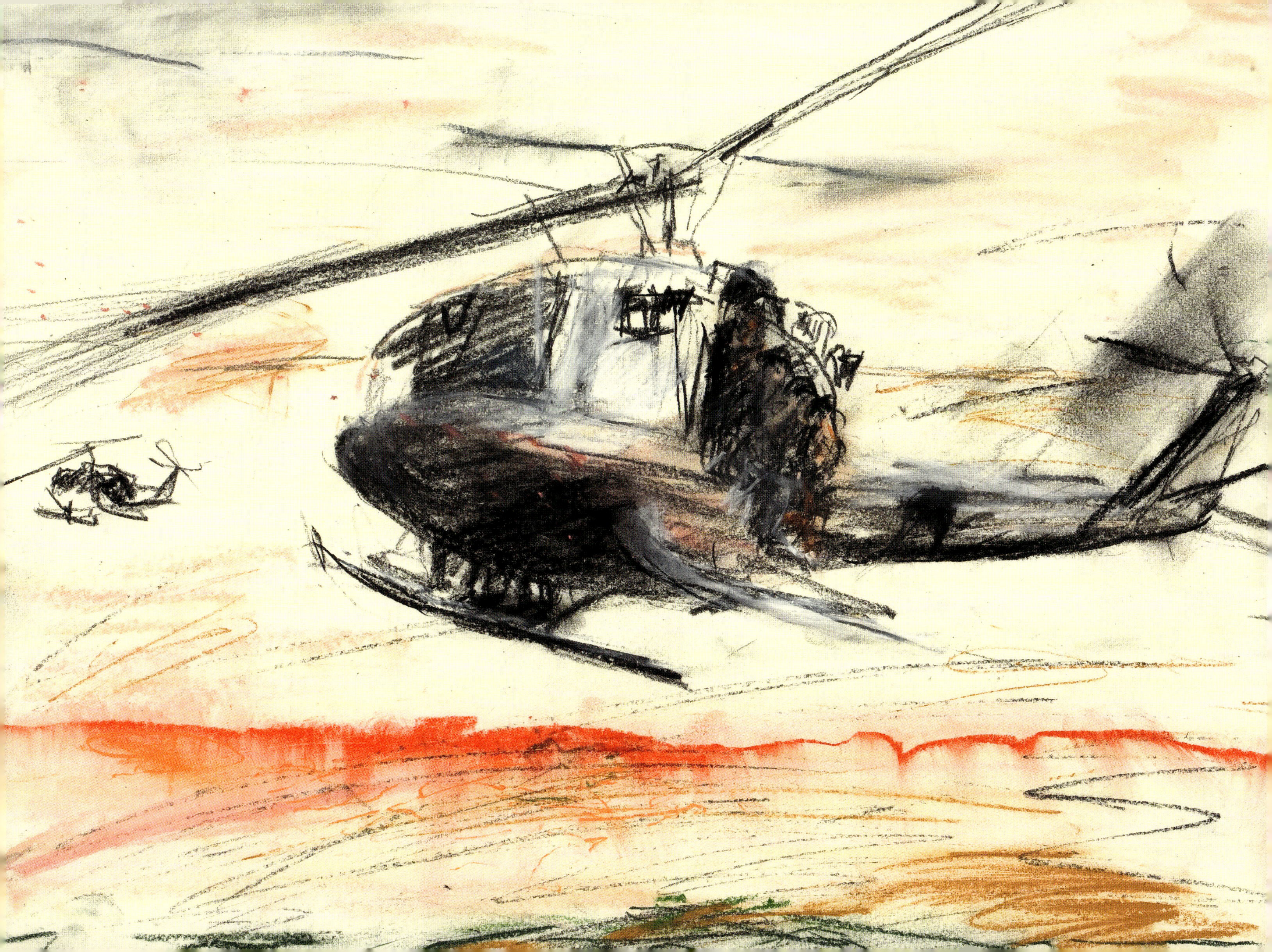

Battlefield, 2012

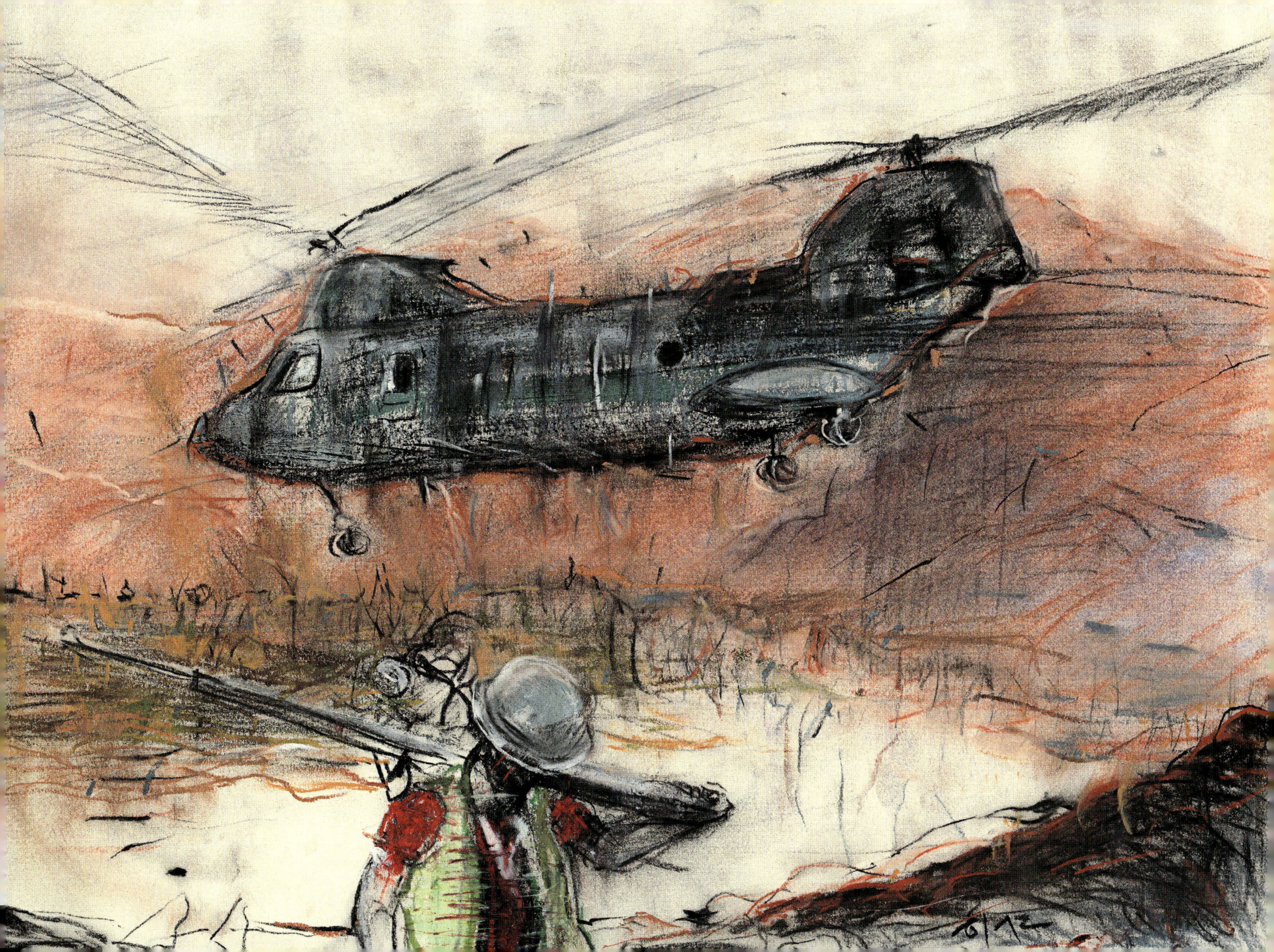

41 Sea Sprite, 2009

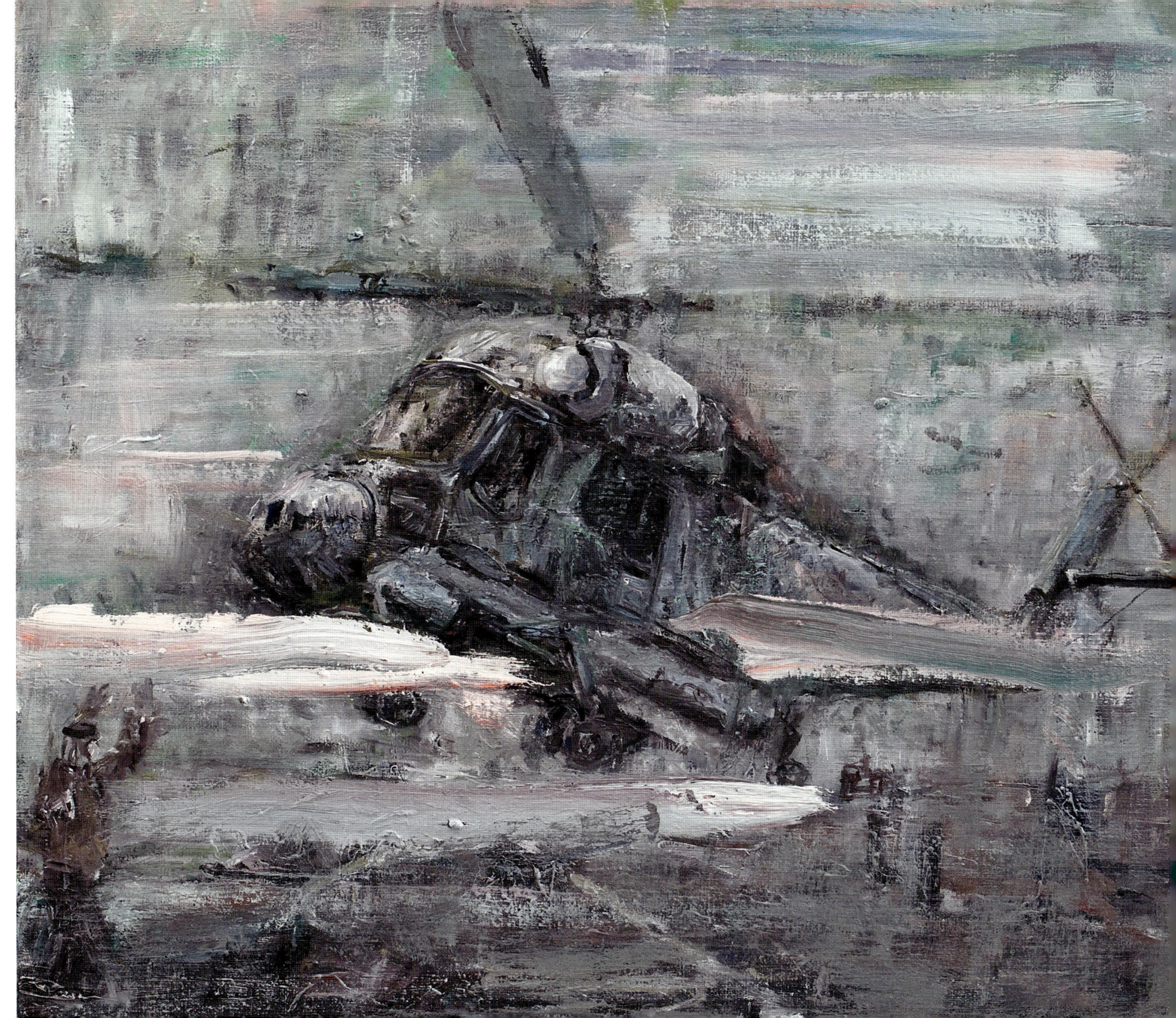

Blue Helicopter, 2010

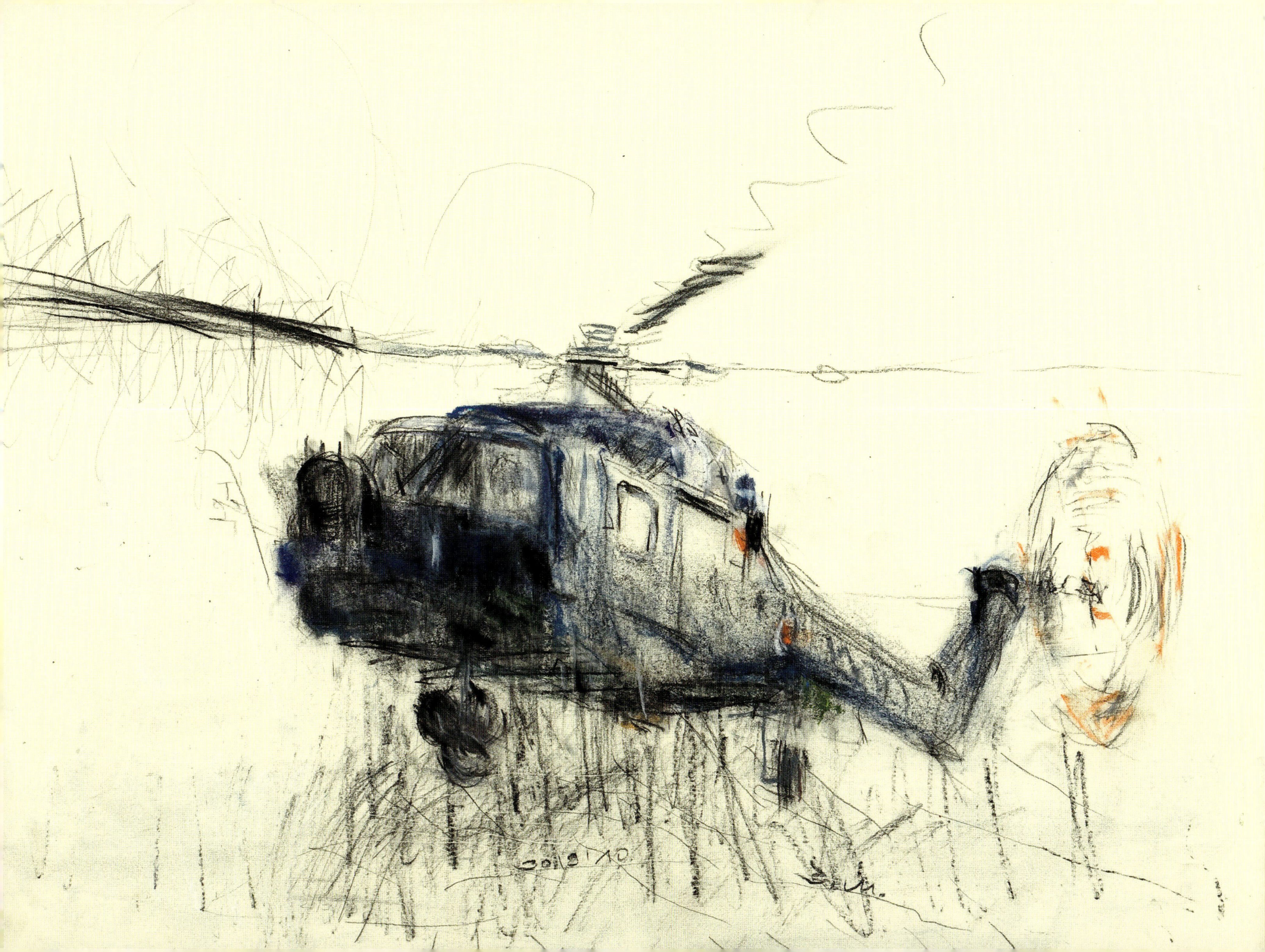

43 Marine, 2009

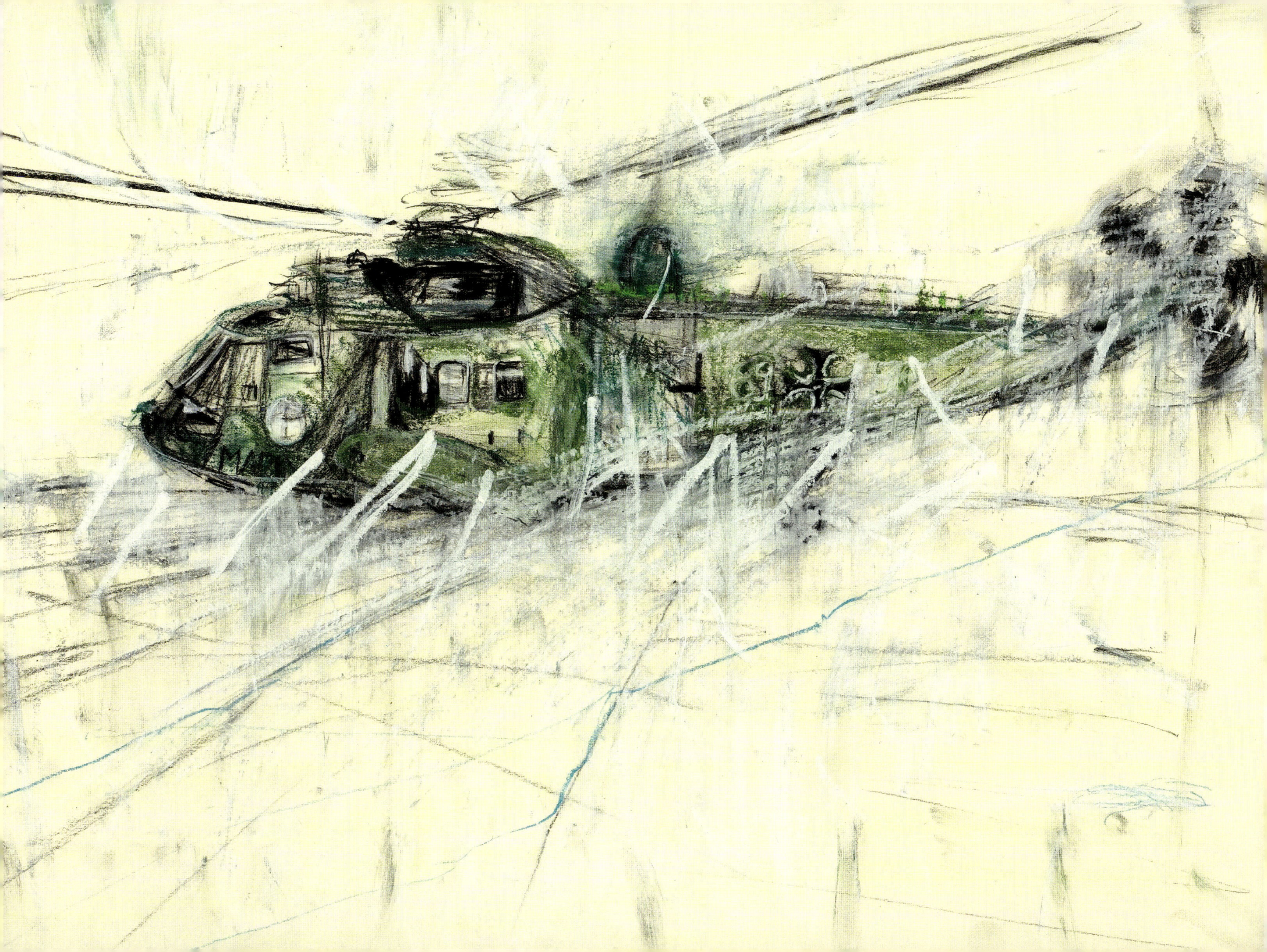

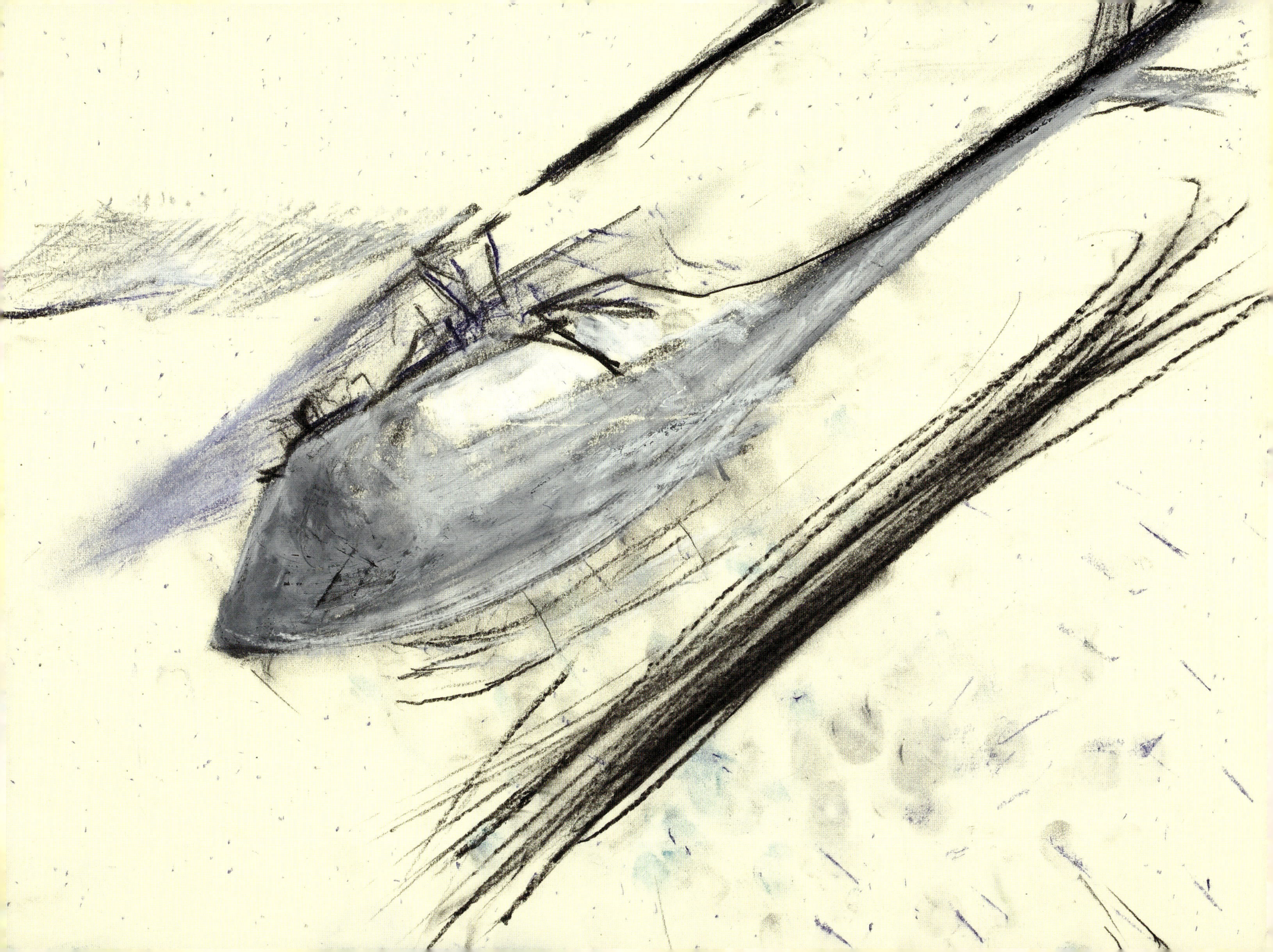

 Ocean II, 2004

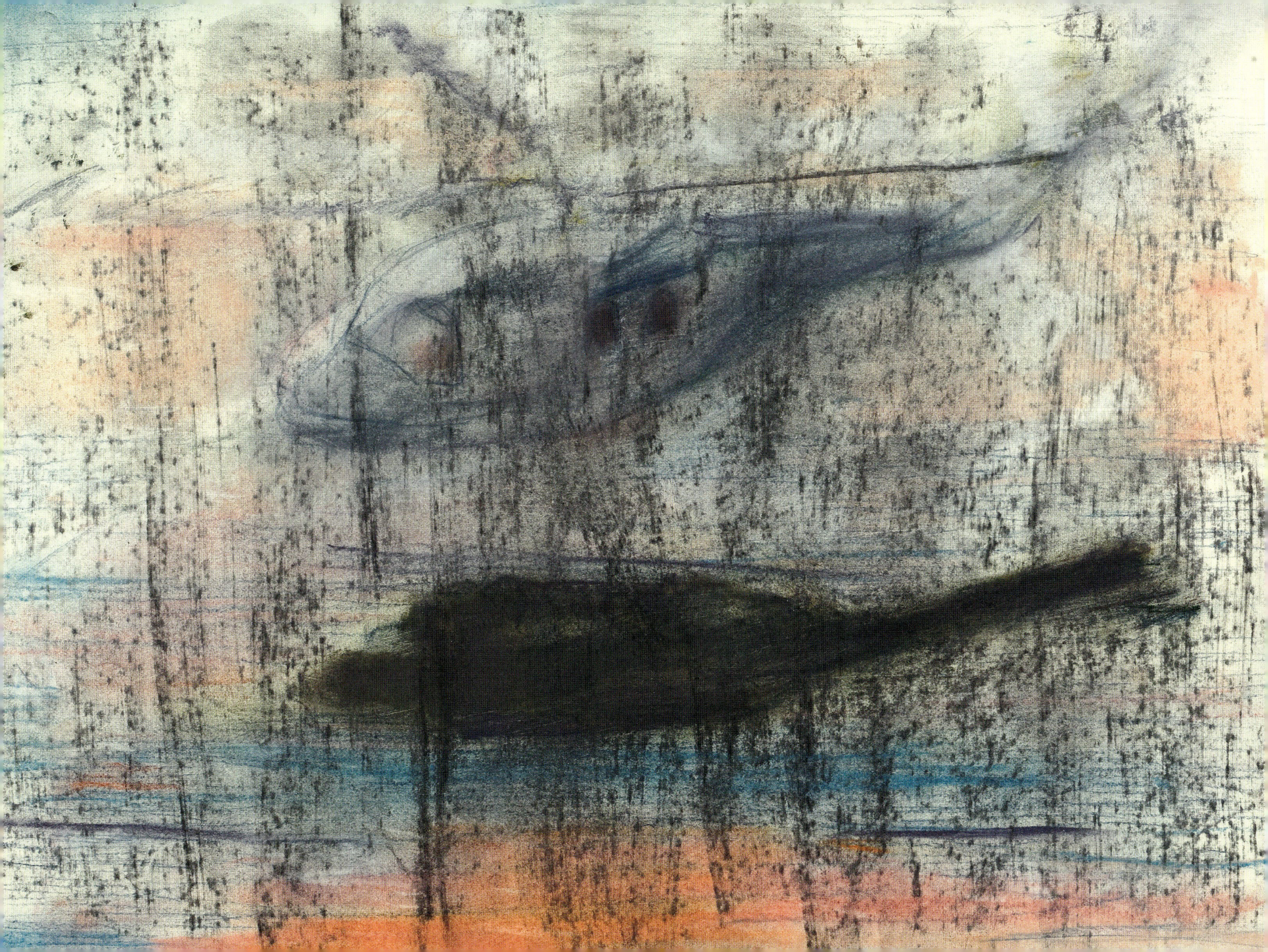

Ocean I, 2004

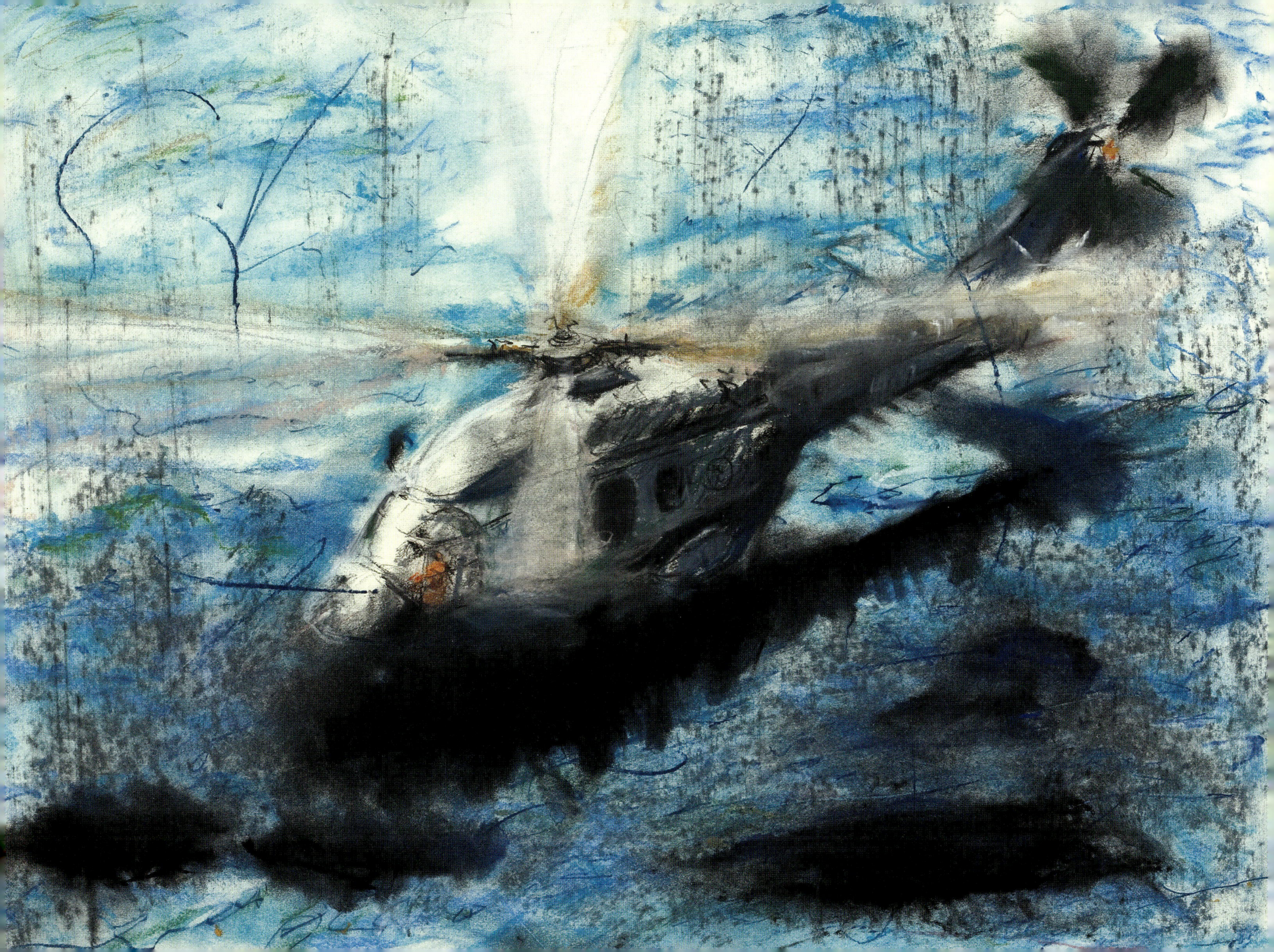

47 Training I, 2004

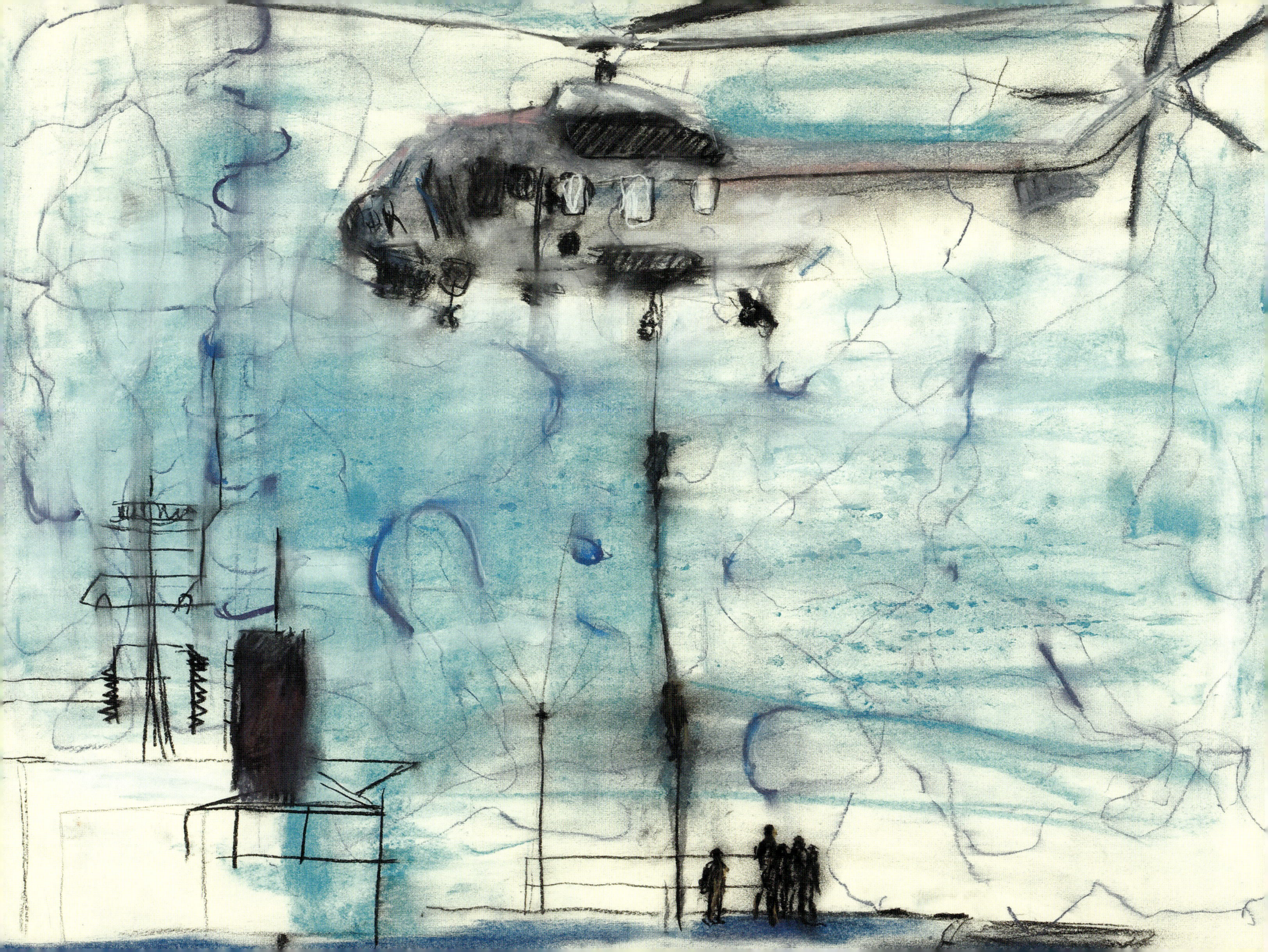

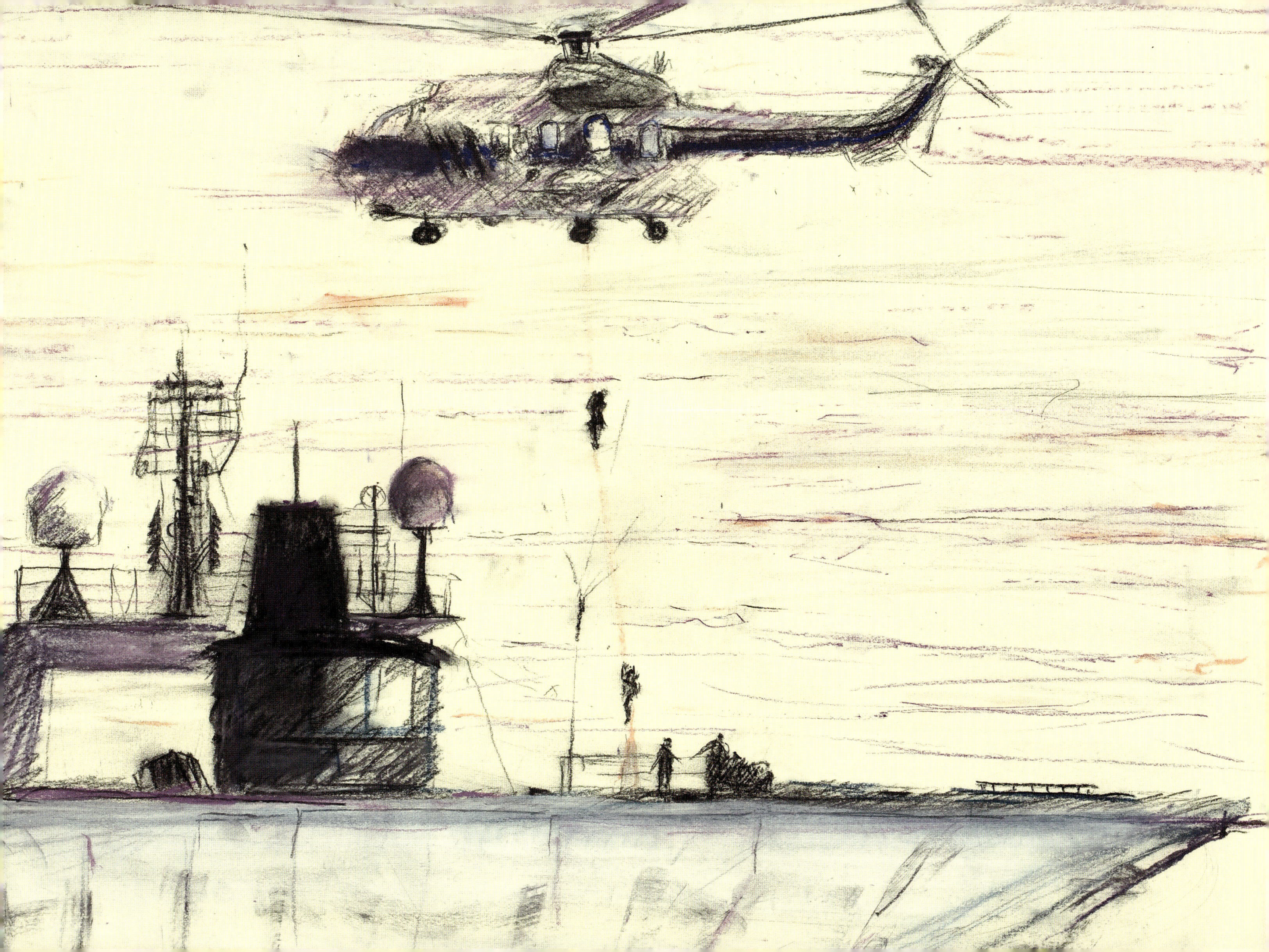

49 Test, 2005

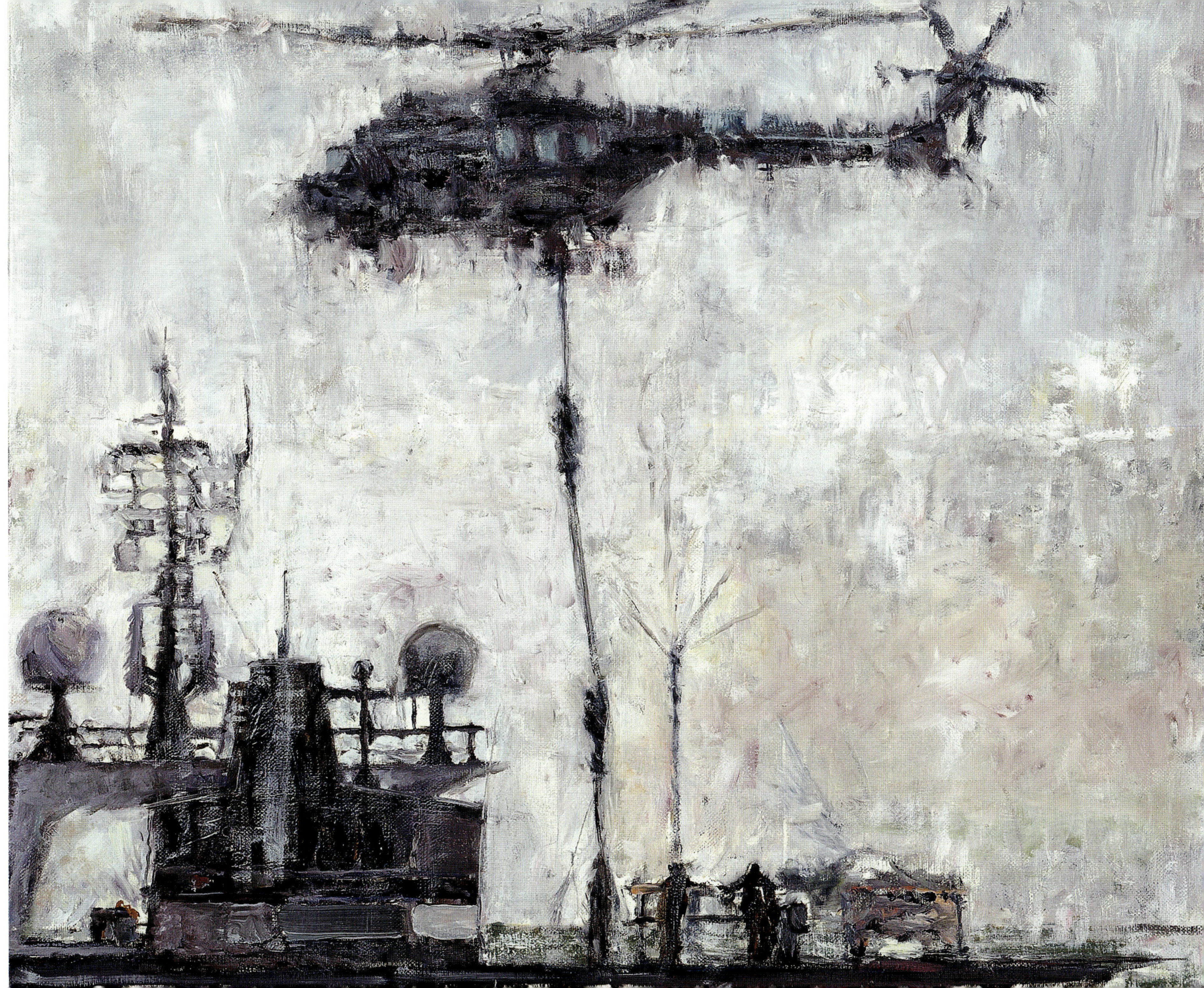

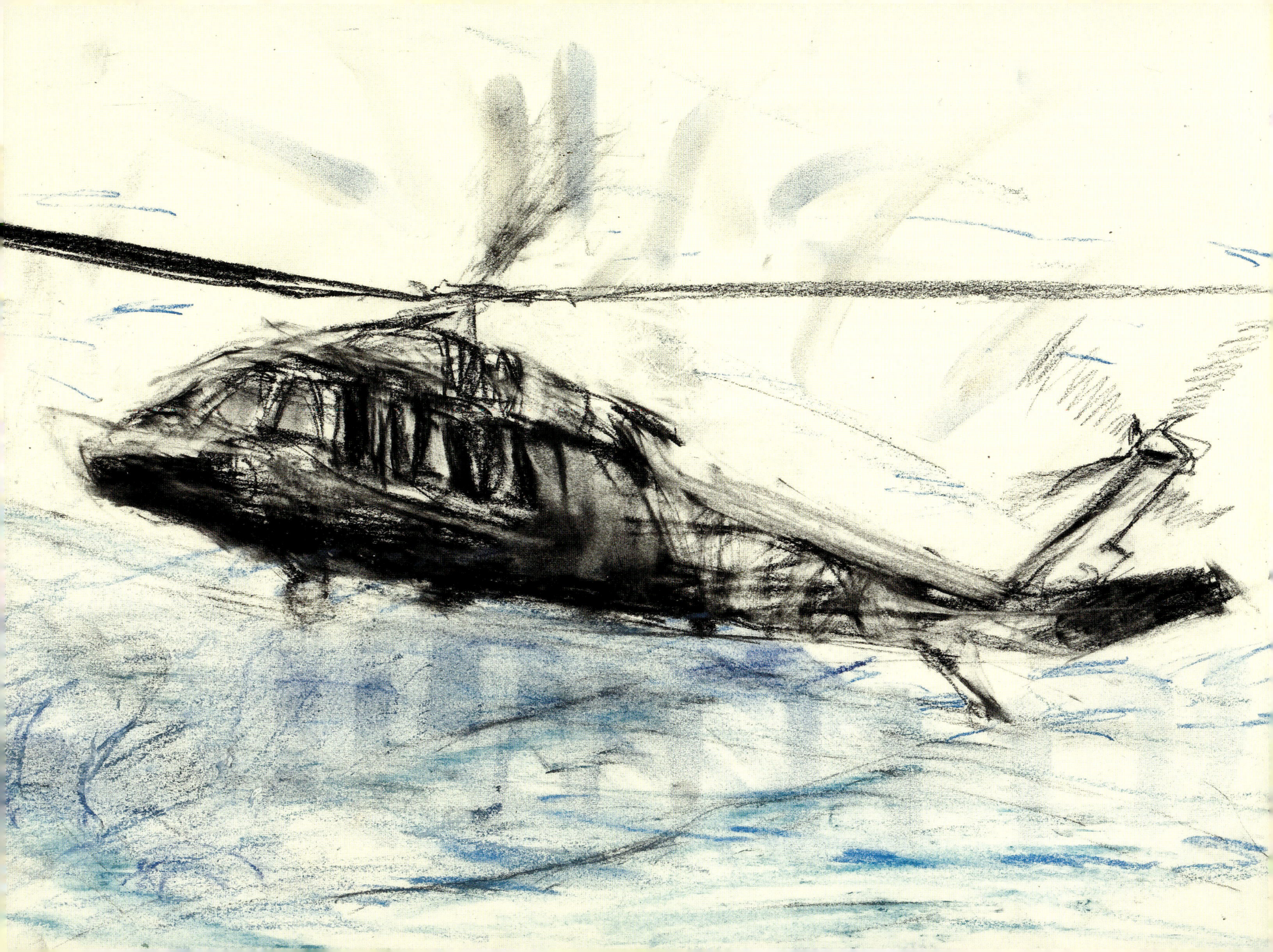

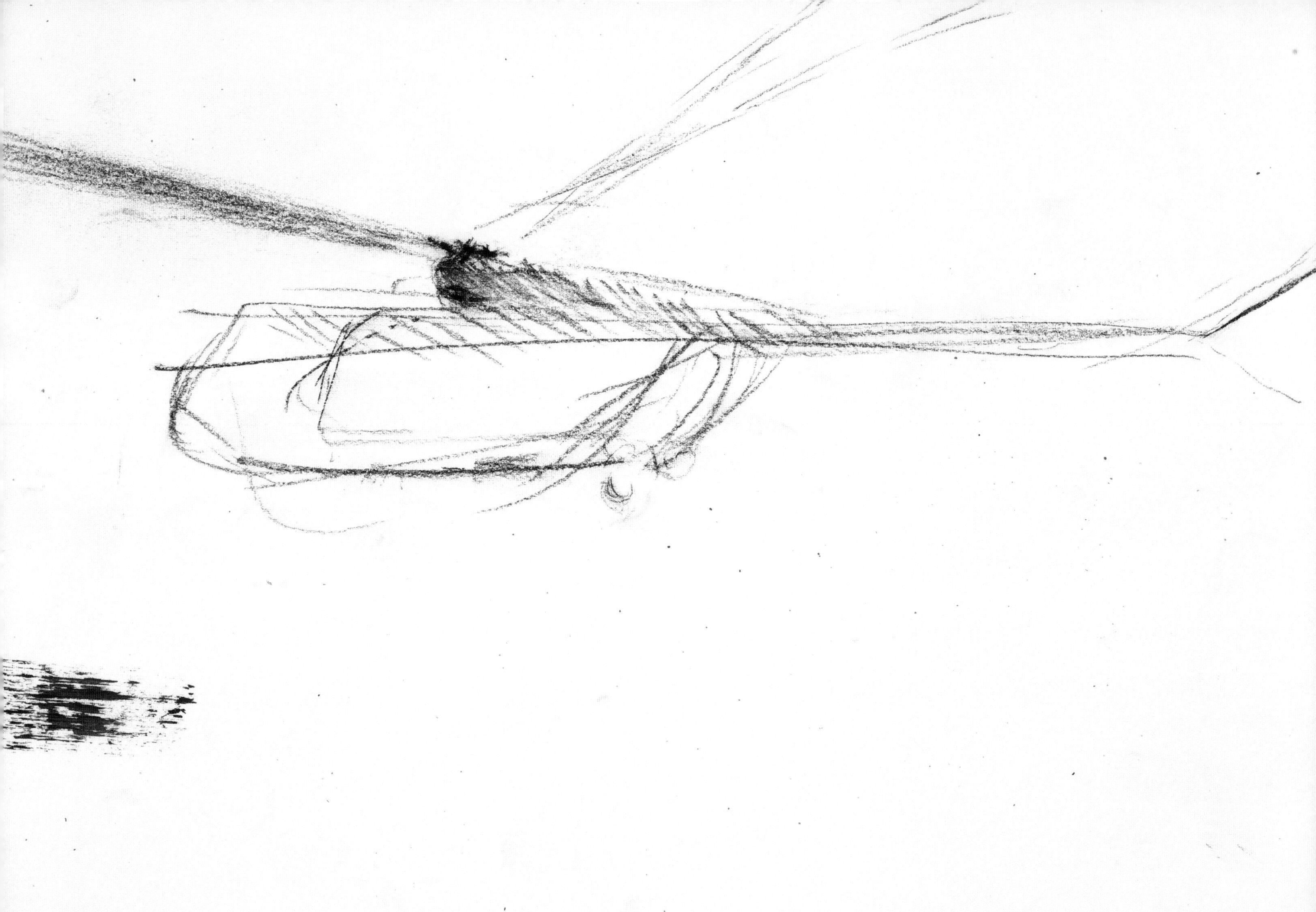

S.M 26/1/05

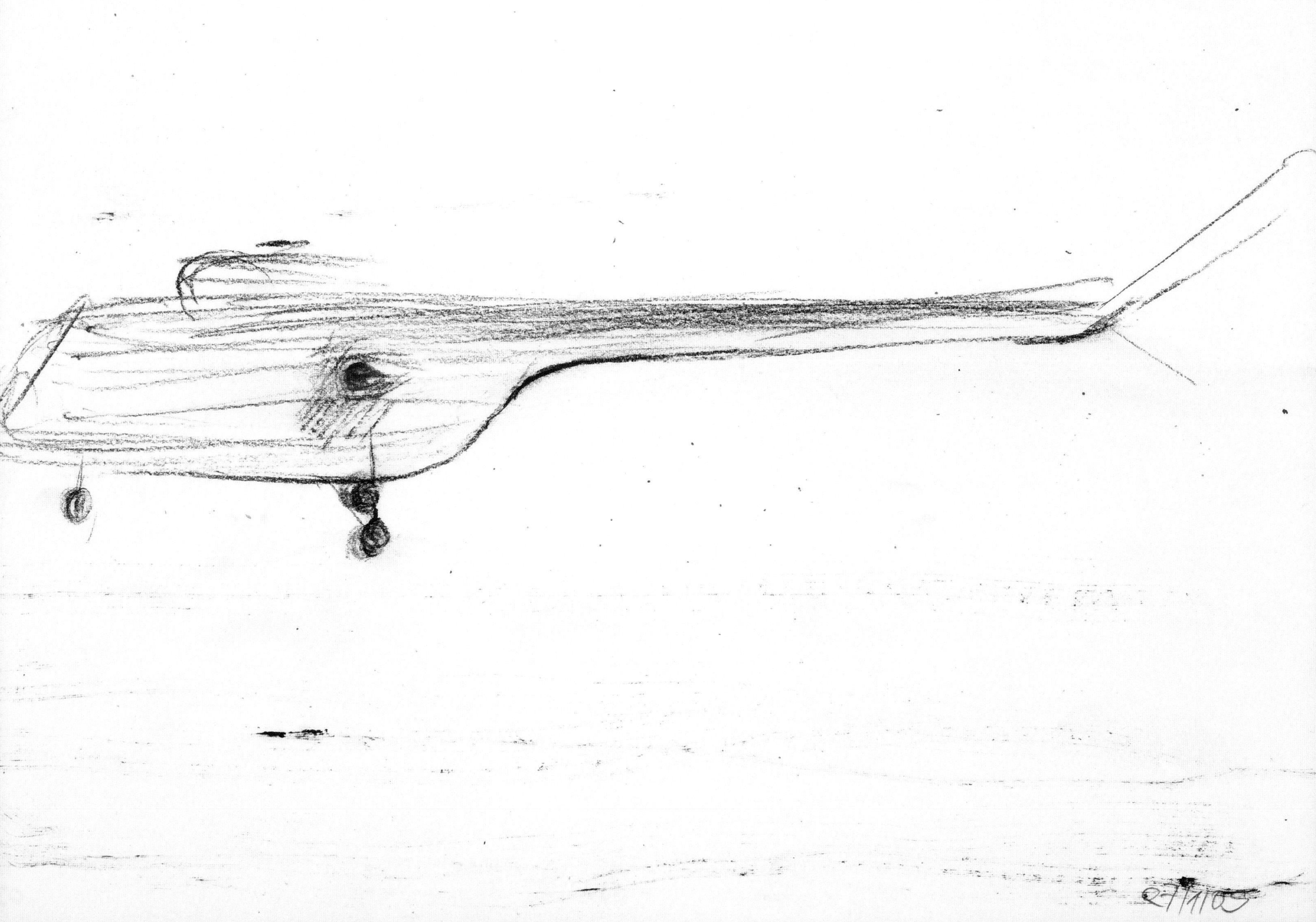

51 Beautiful Helicopter I, 2009

52 Beautiful Helicopter II, 2009

53 Black, 2009

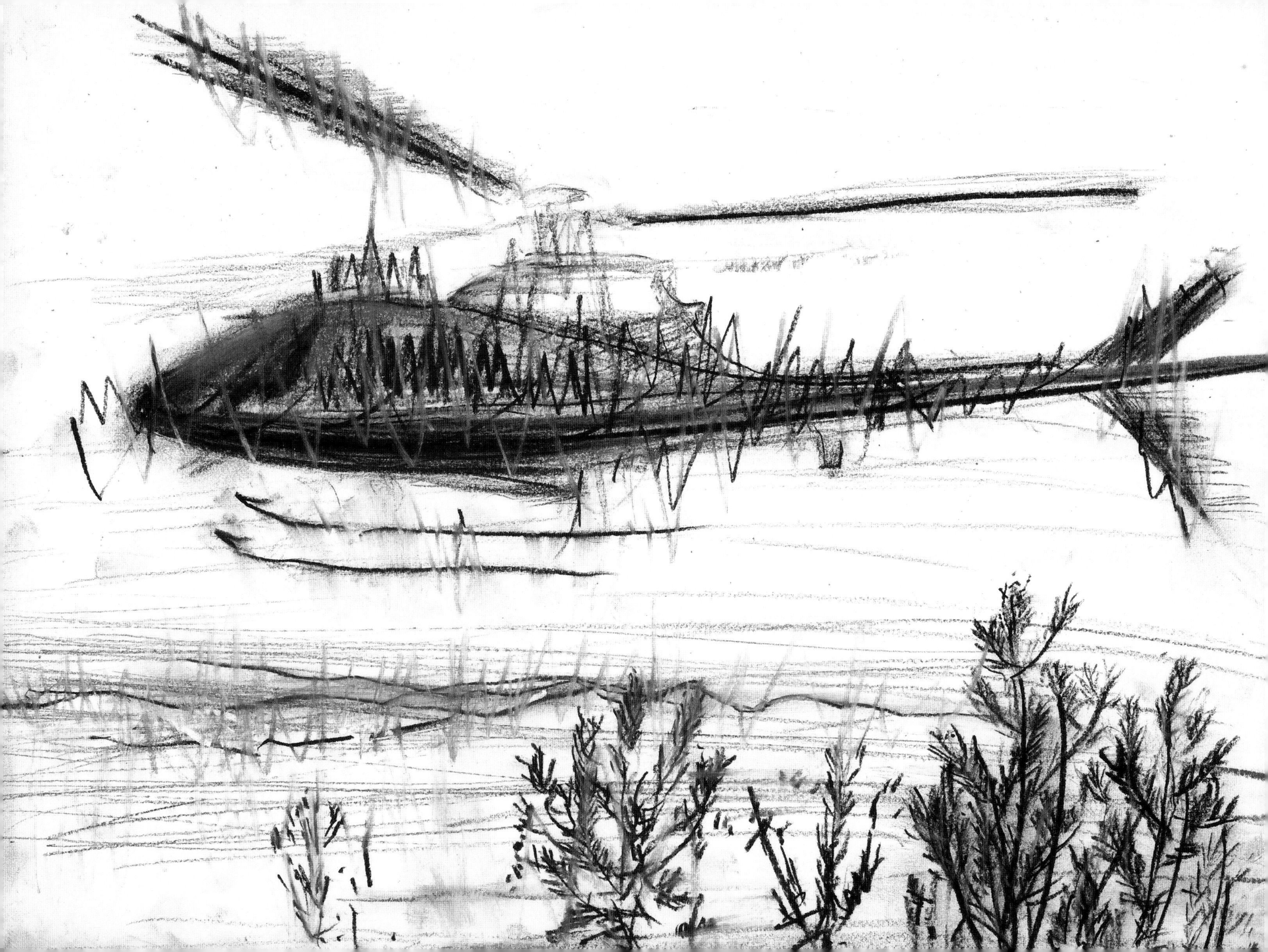

 Waldhubschrauber VI, 2006

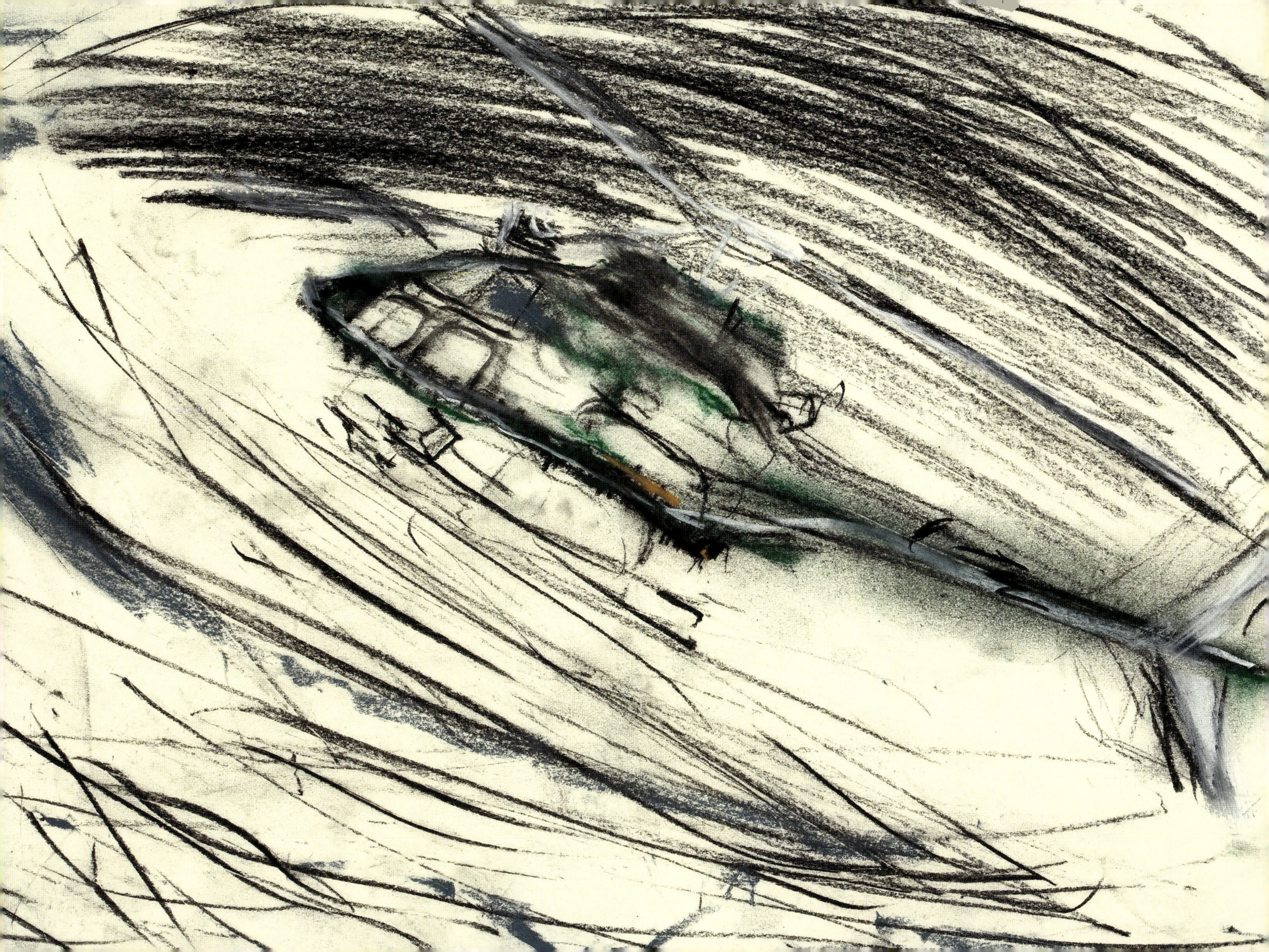

55 Waldhubschrauber III, 2006

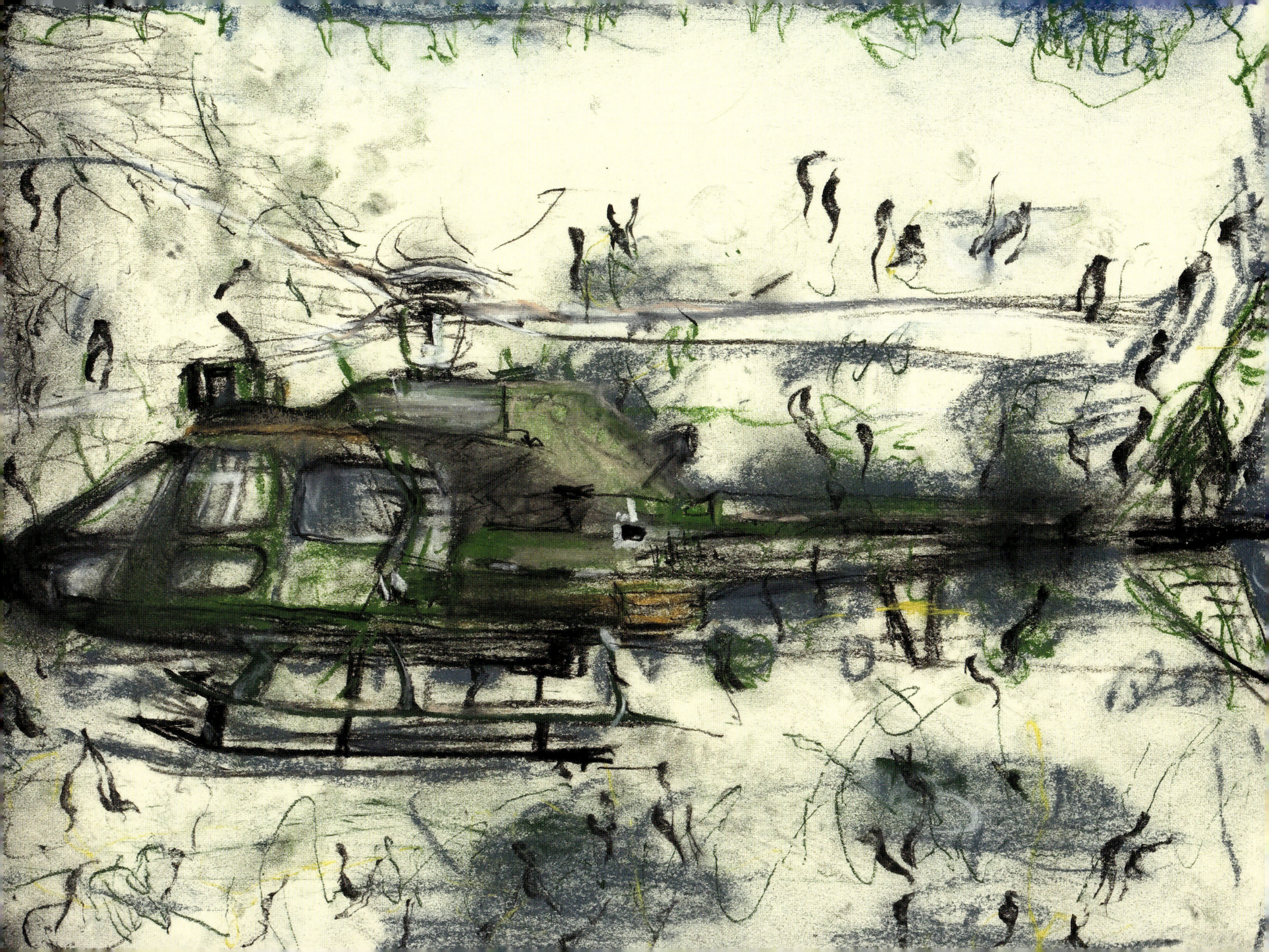

Waldhubschrauber II, 2006

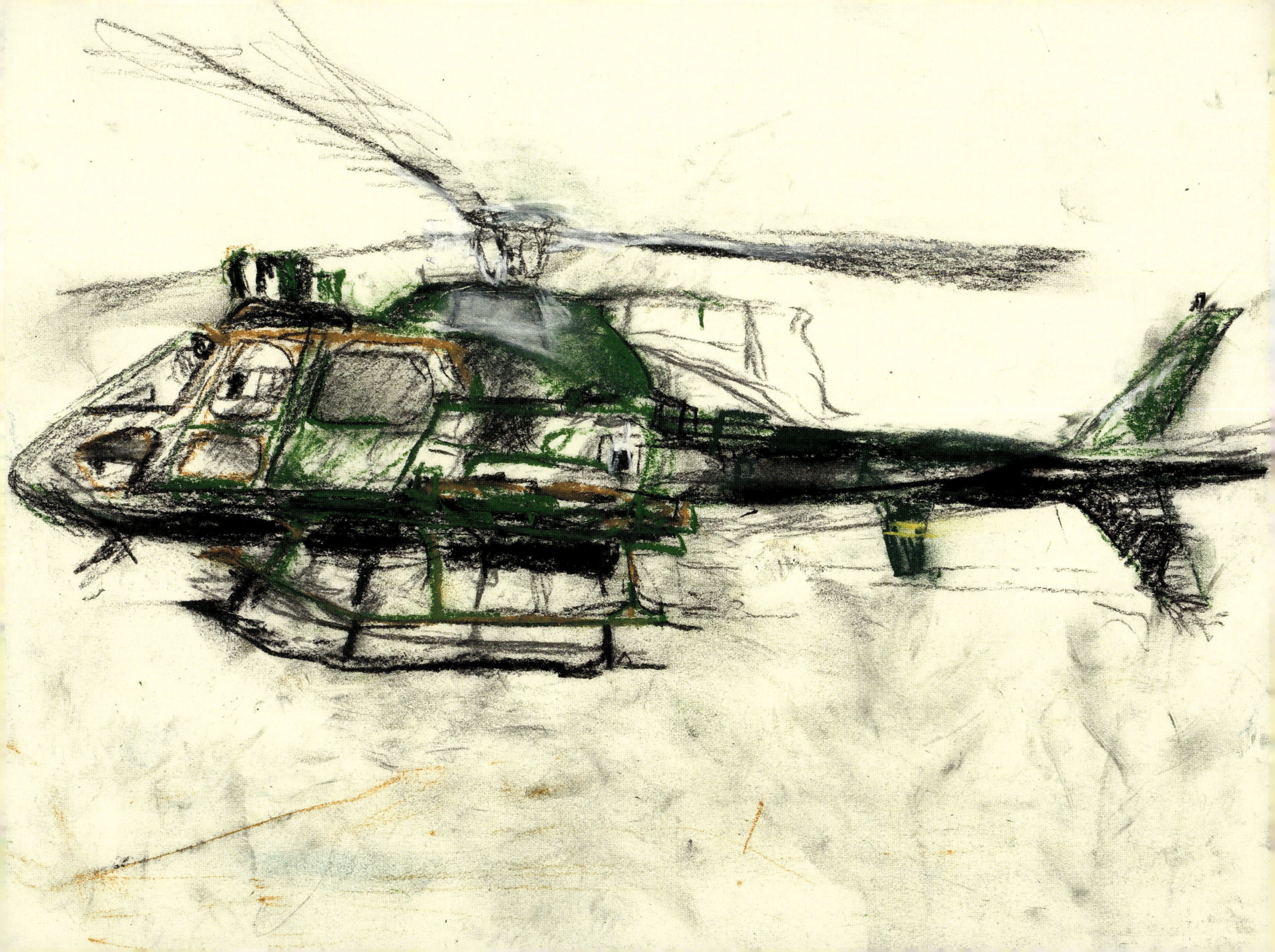

57 Waldhubschrauber I, 2006

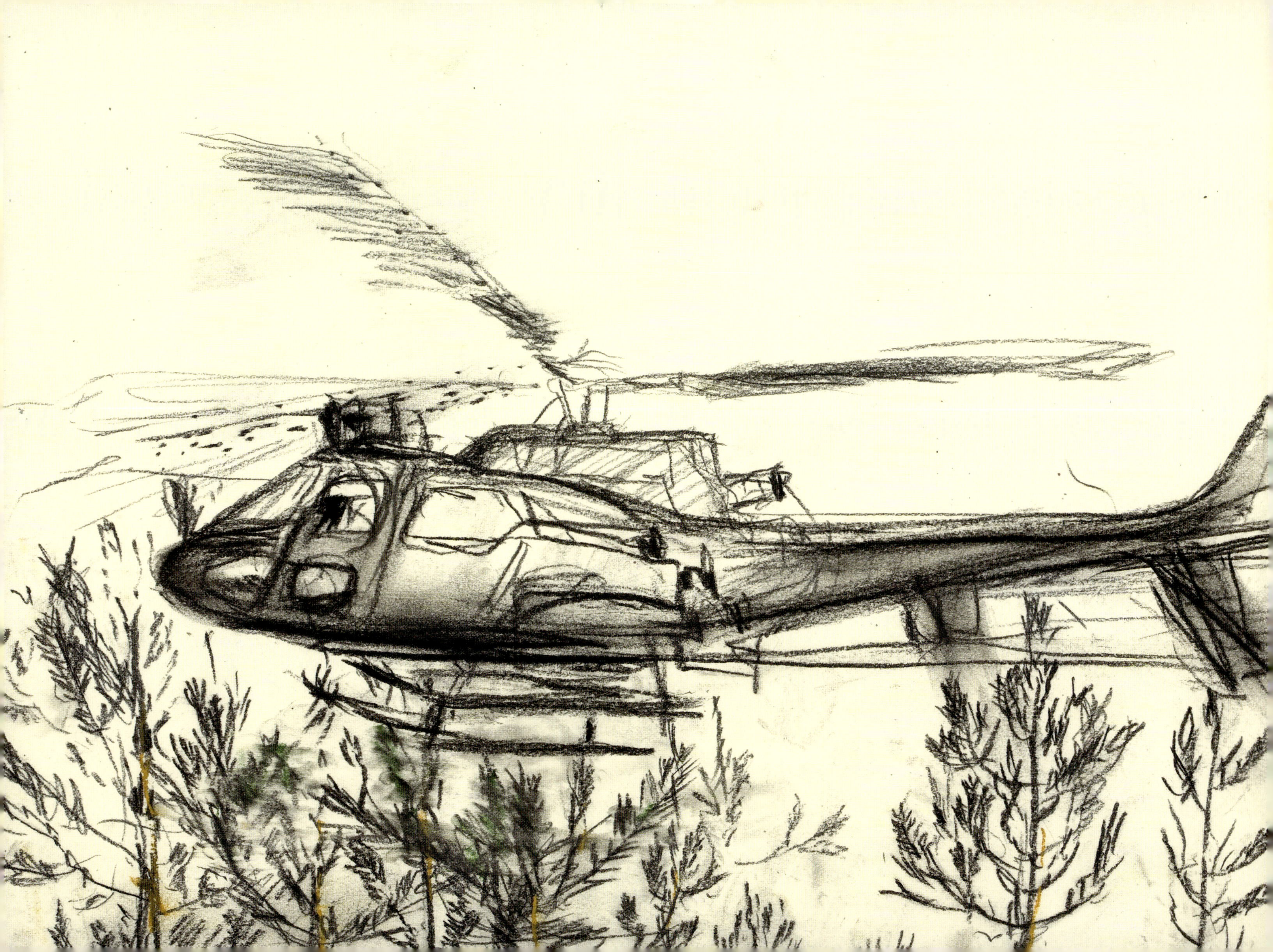

Embassy, 2004

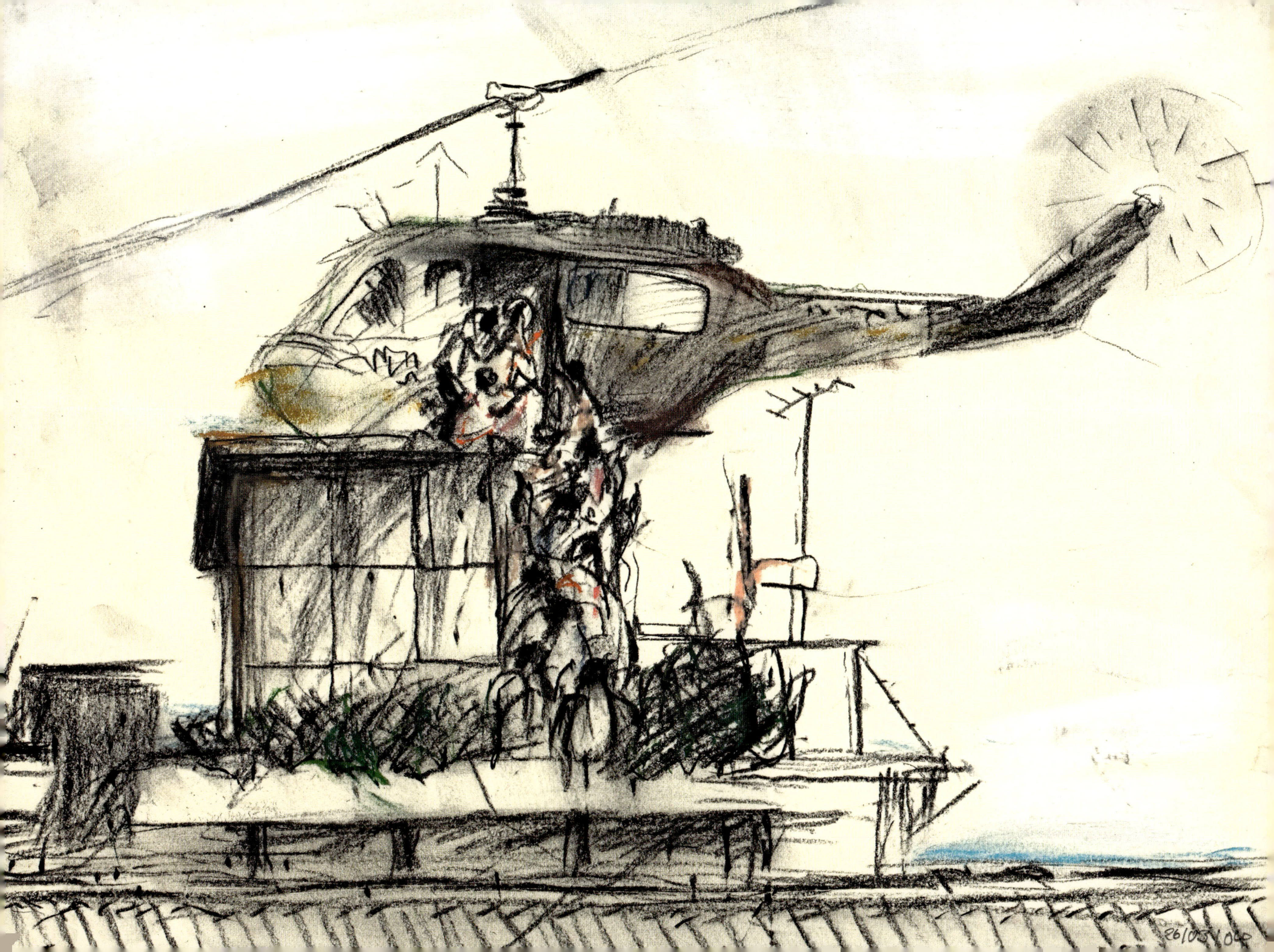

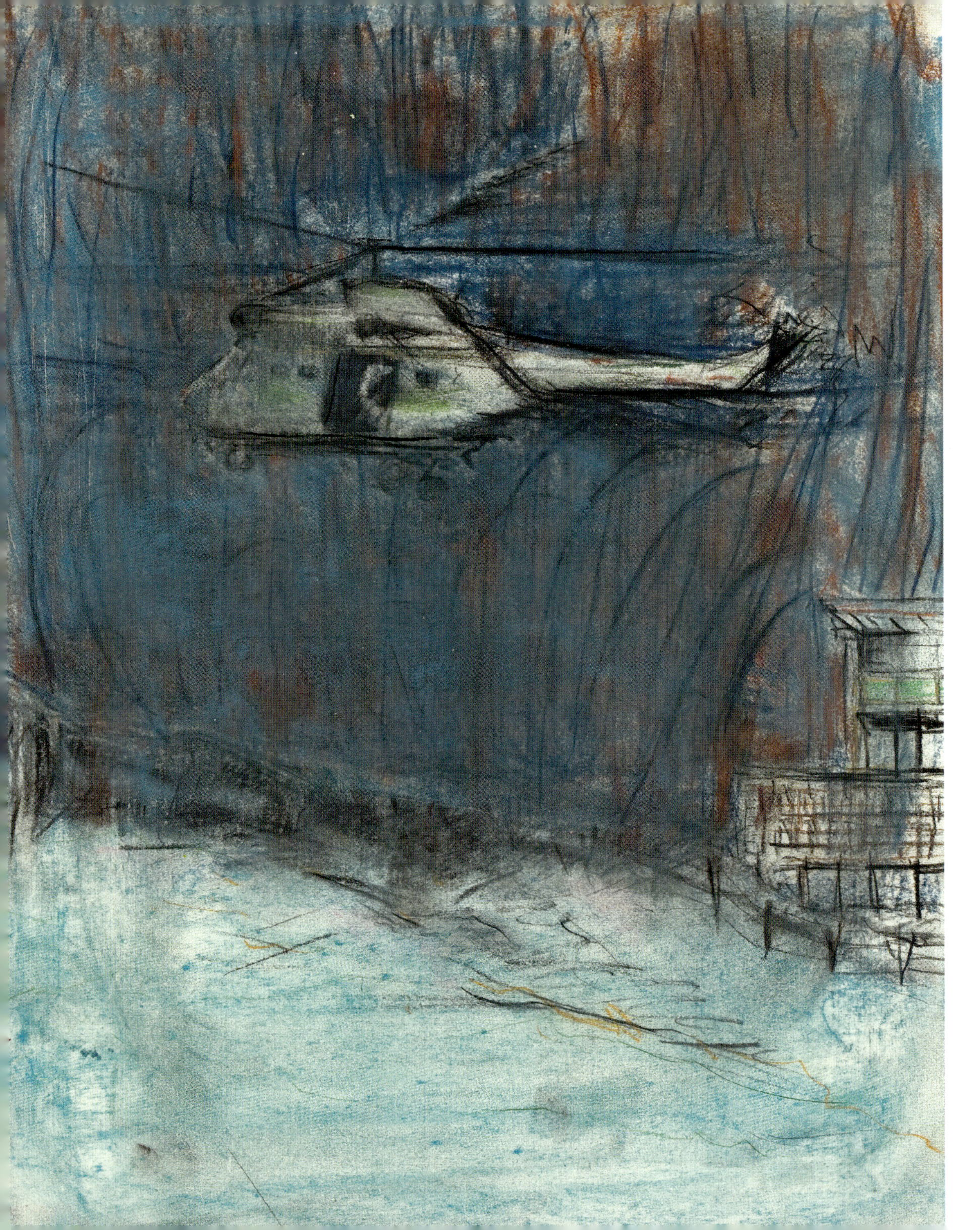

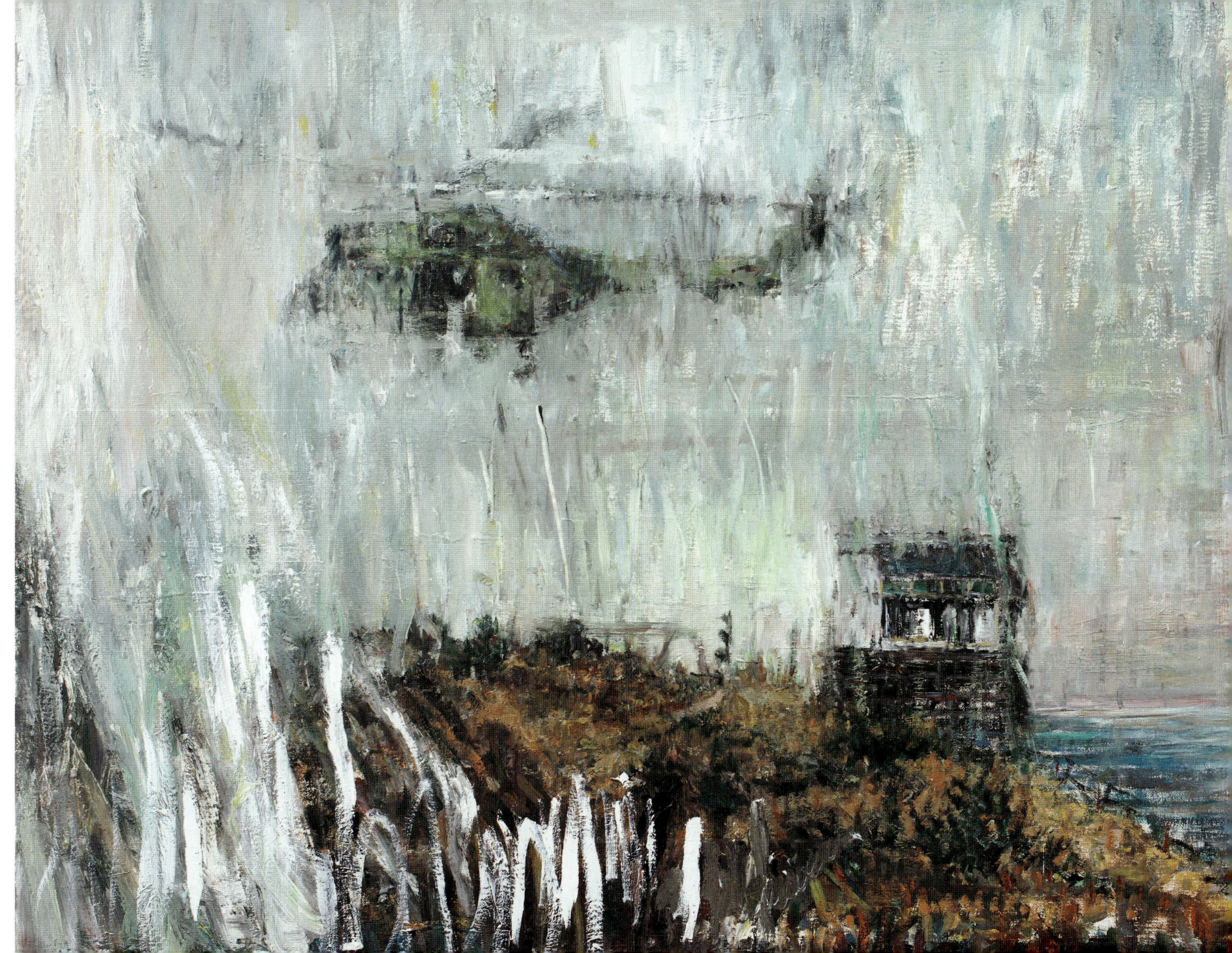

59 Border Checkpoint, 2011

60 Border, 2013

61 Ice Wall, 2011

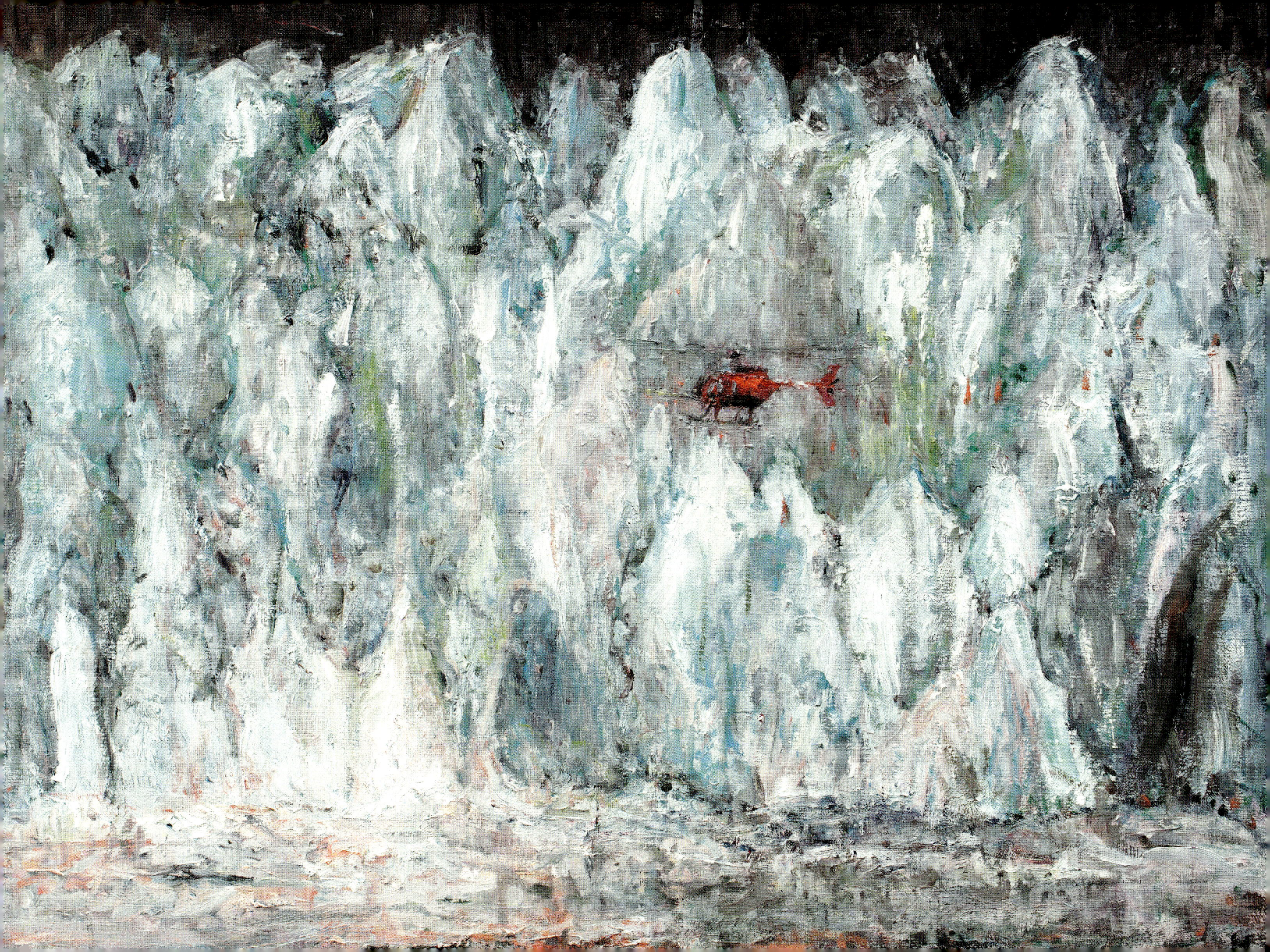

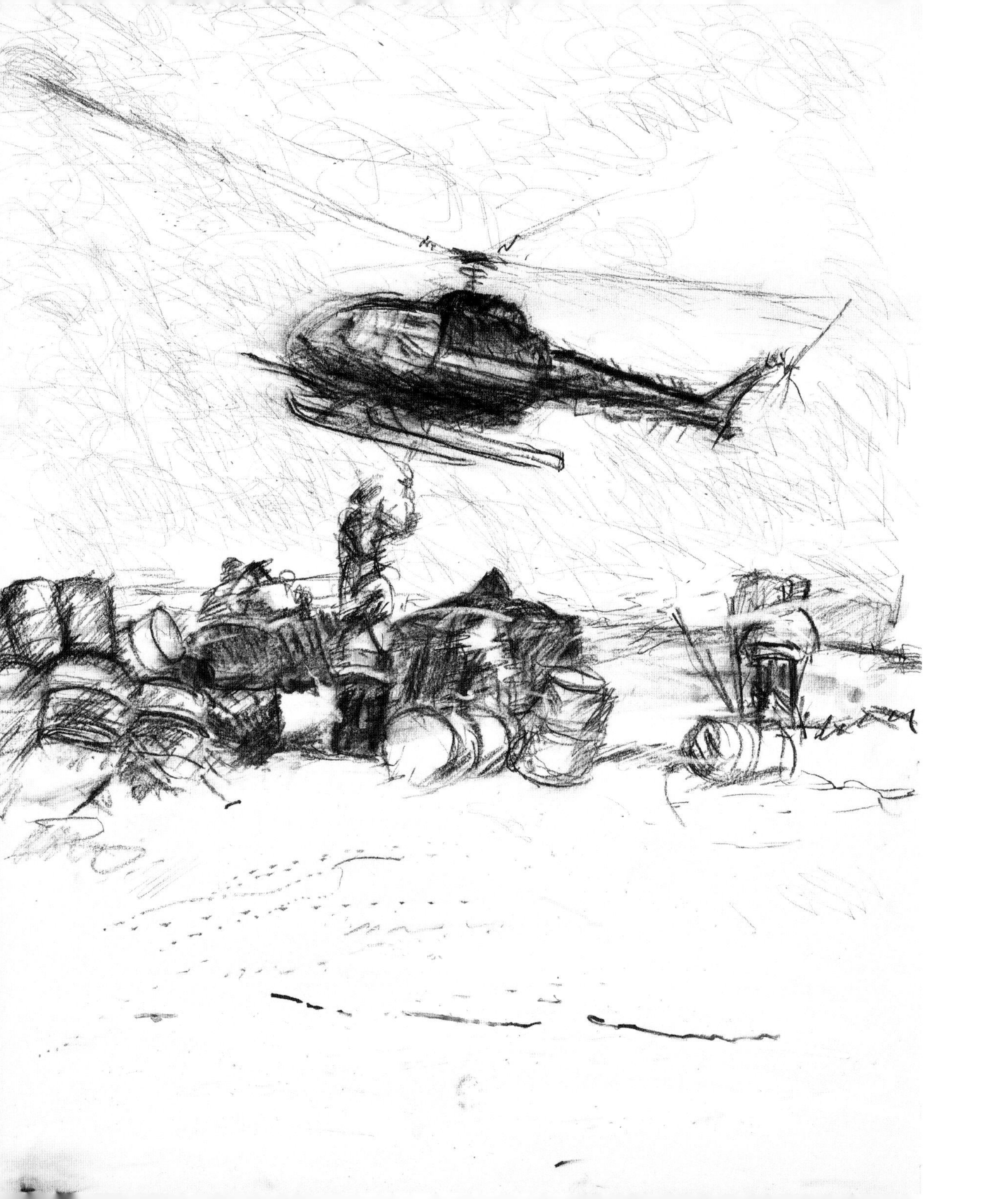

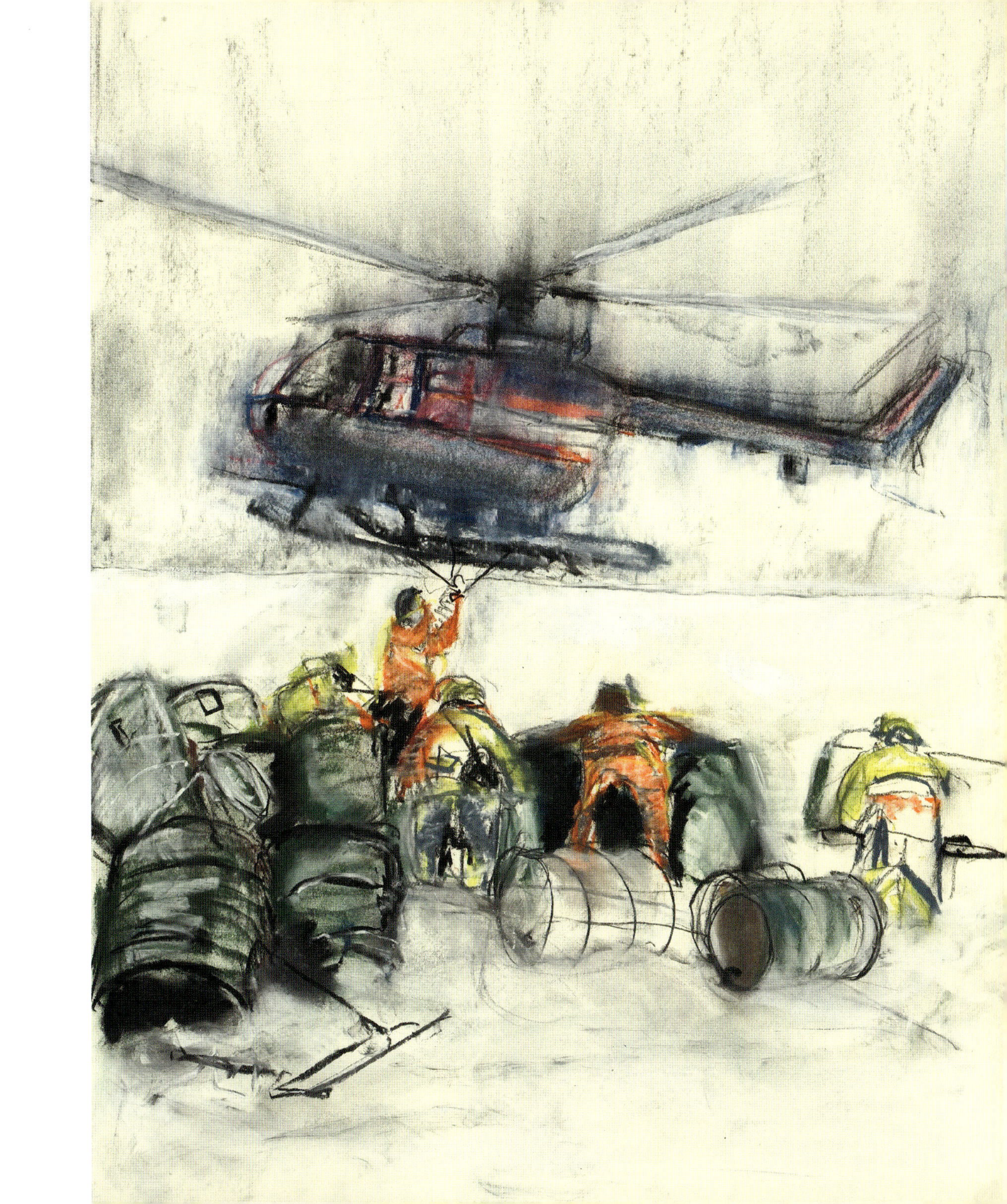

62 North Pole I, 2004

63 North Pole II, 2004

64 North Pole, 2005

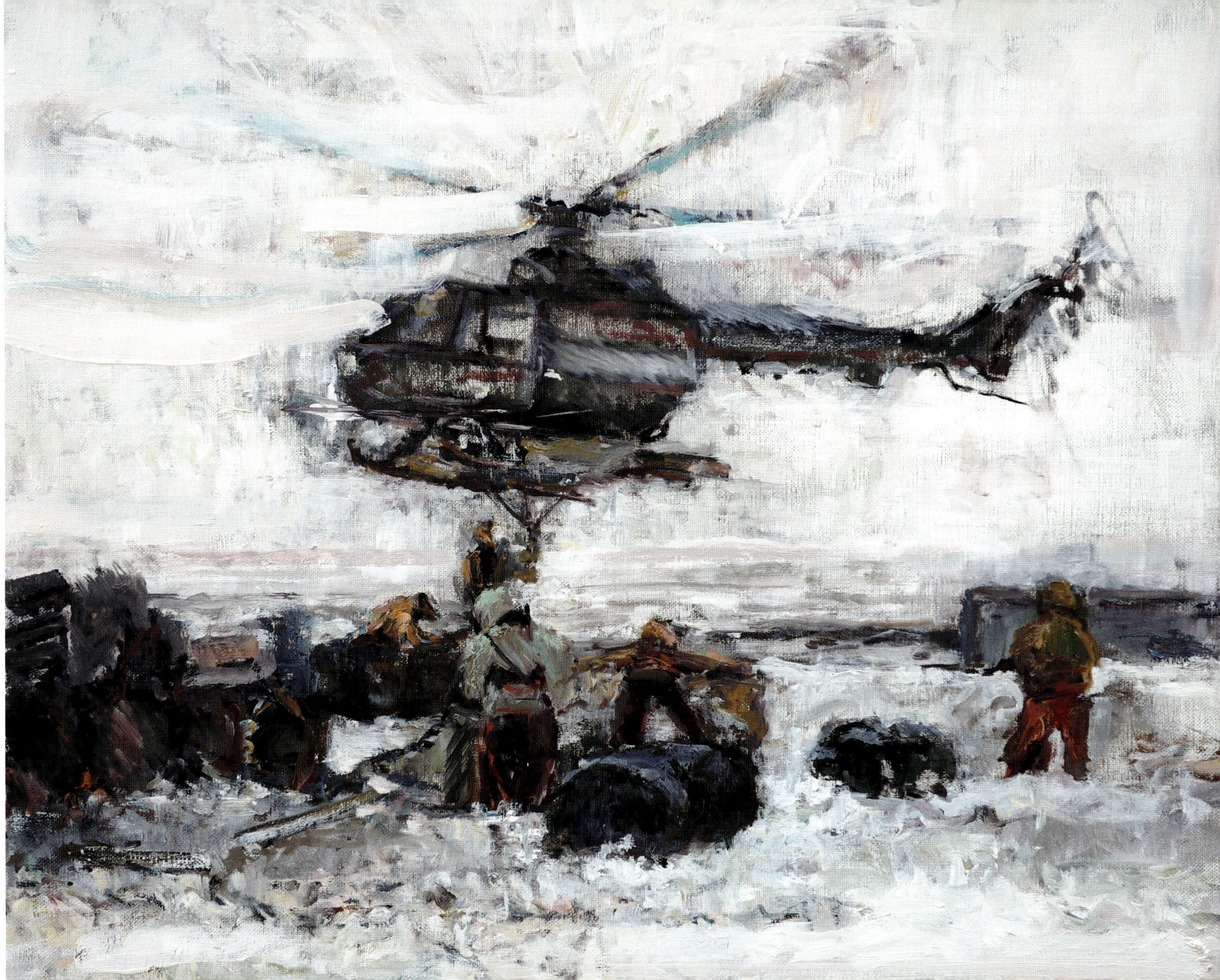

65 Sea King, (detail), 2007

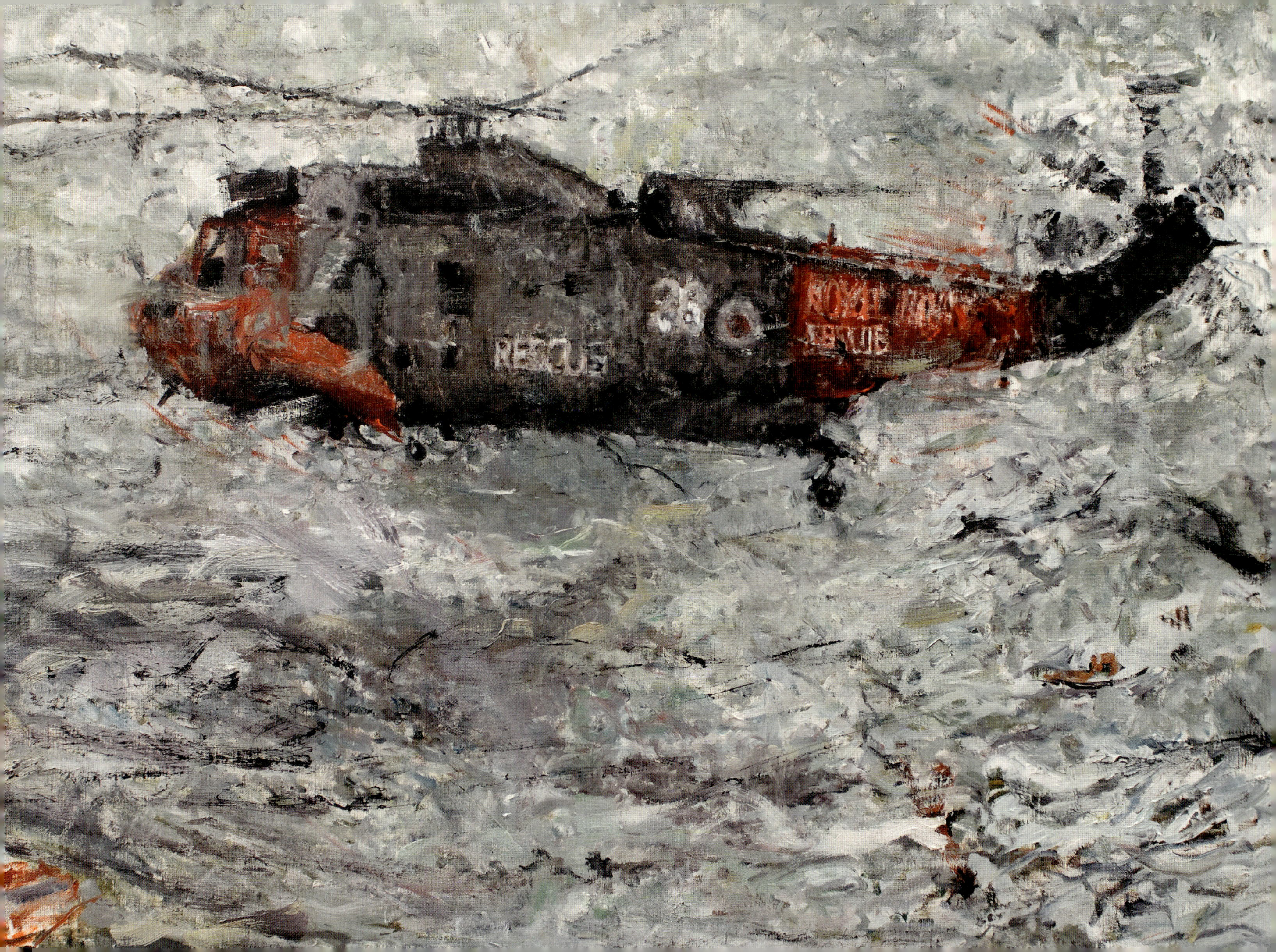
RESCUE

 Sea King (Rain), 2013

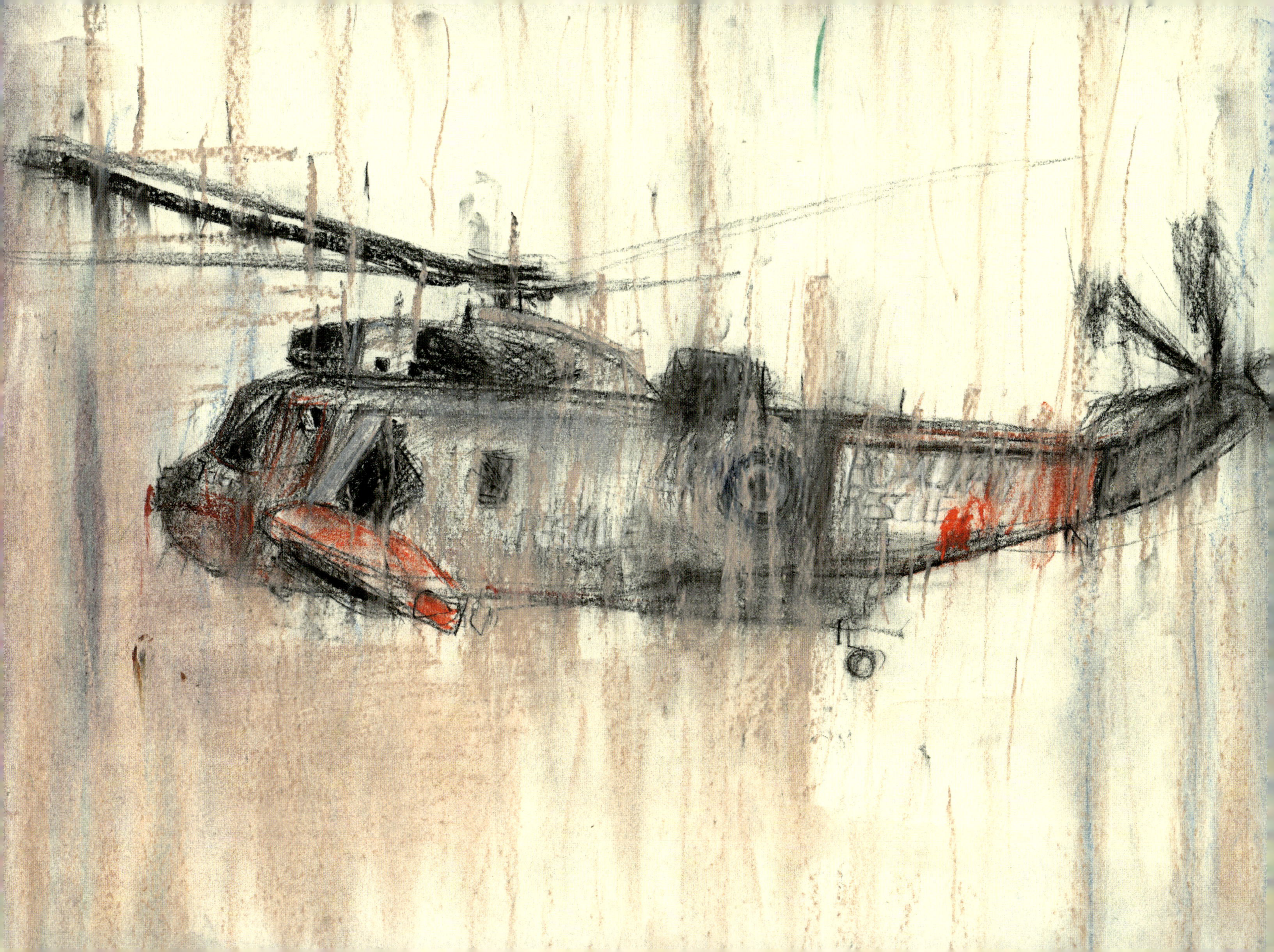

 Rescue, 2013

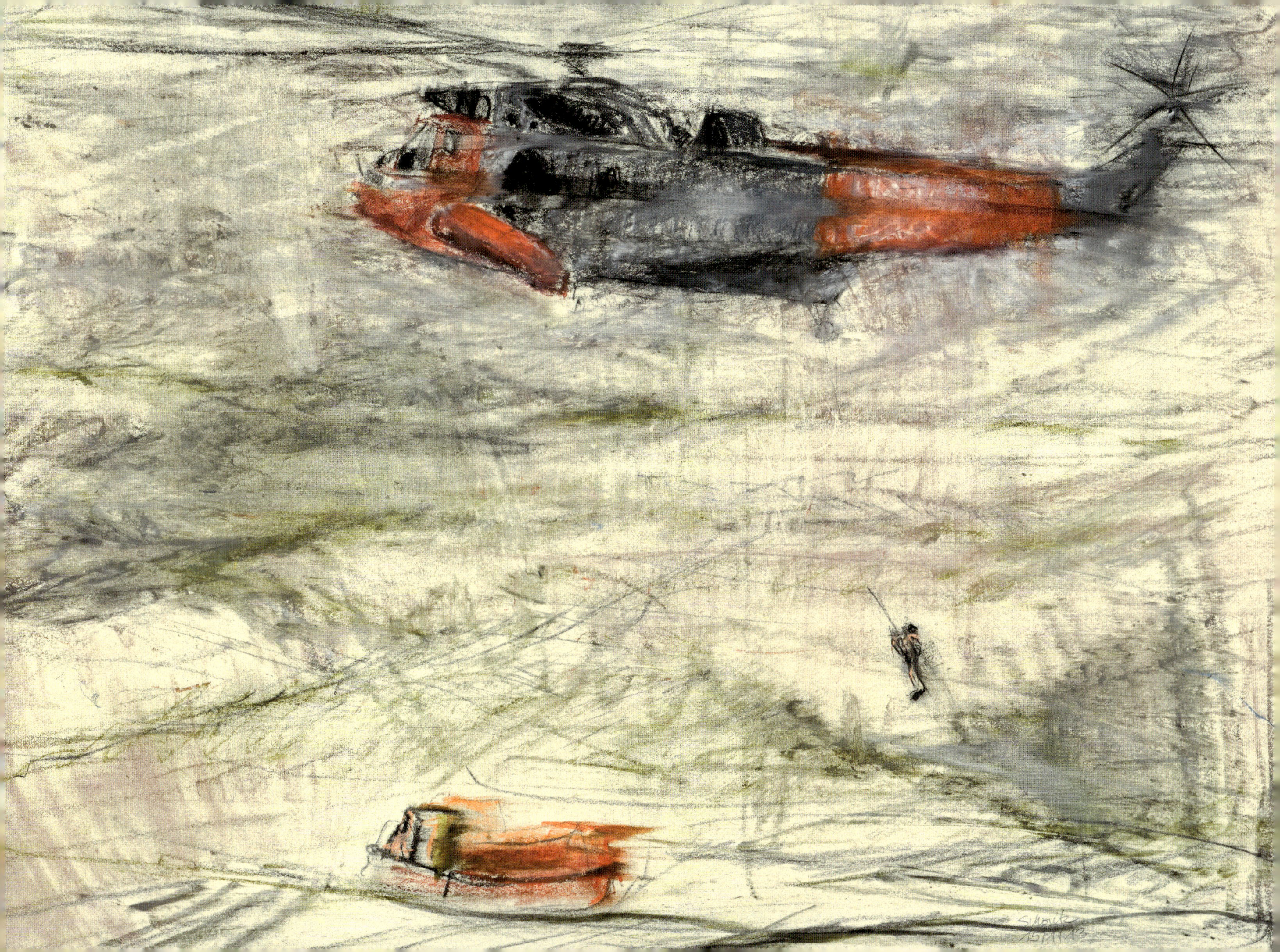

Terrain III, 2009

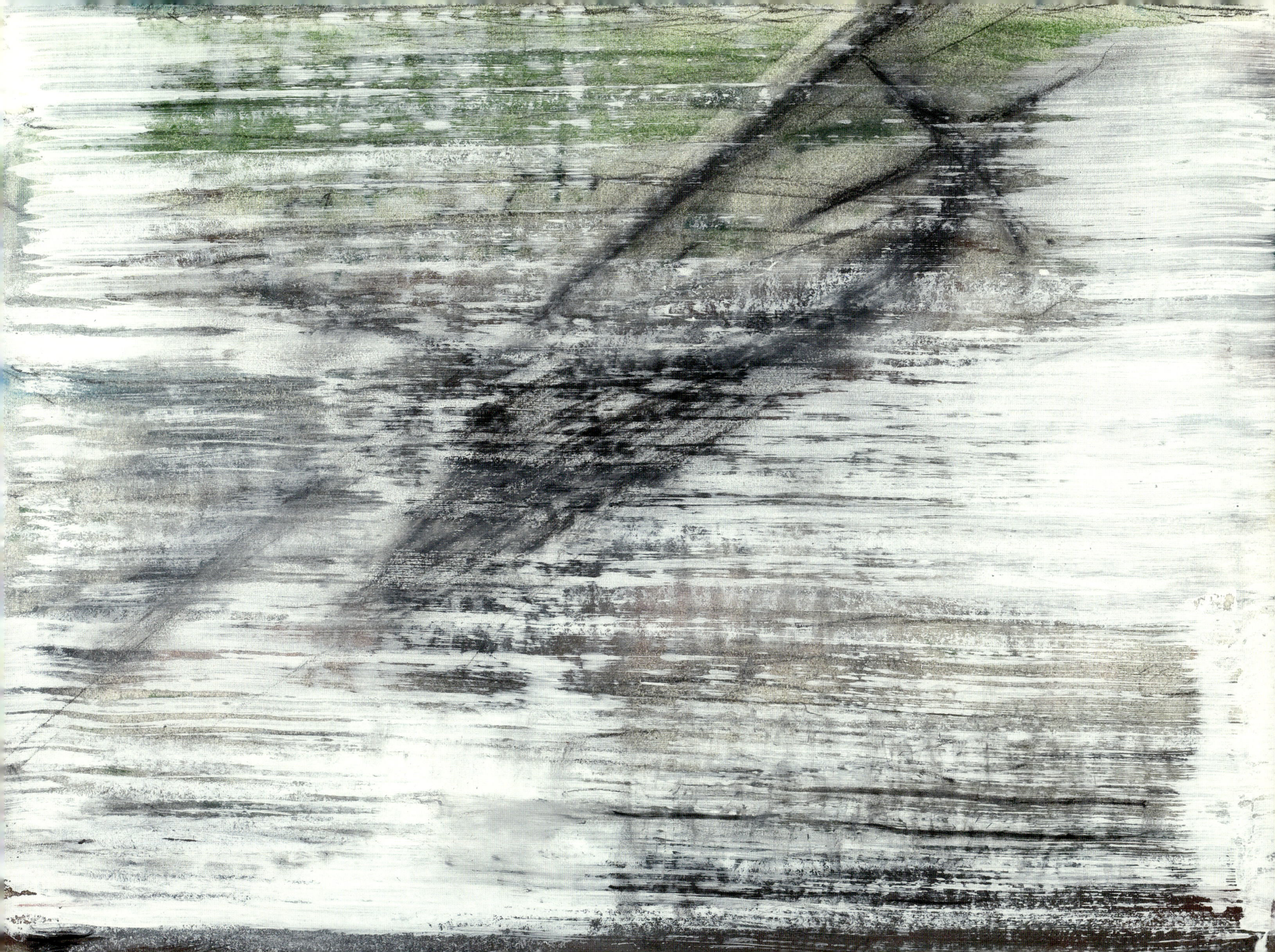

69 Terrain I, 2004

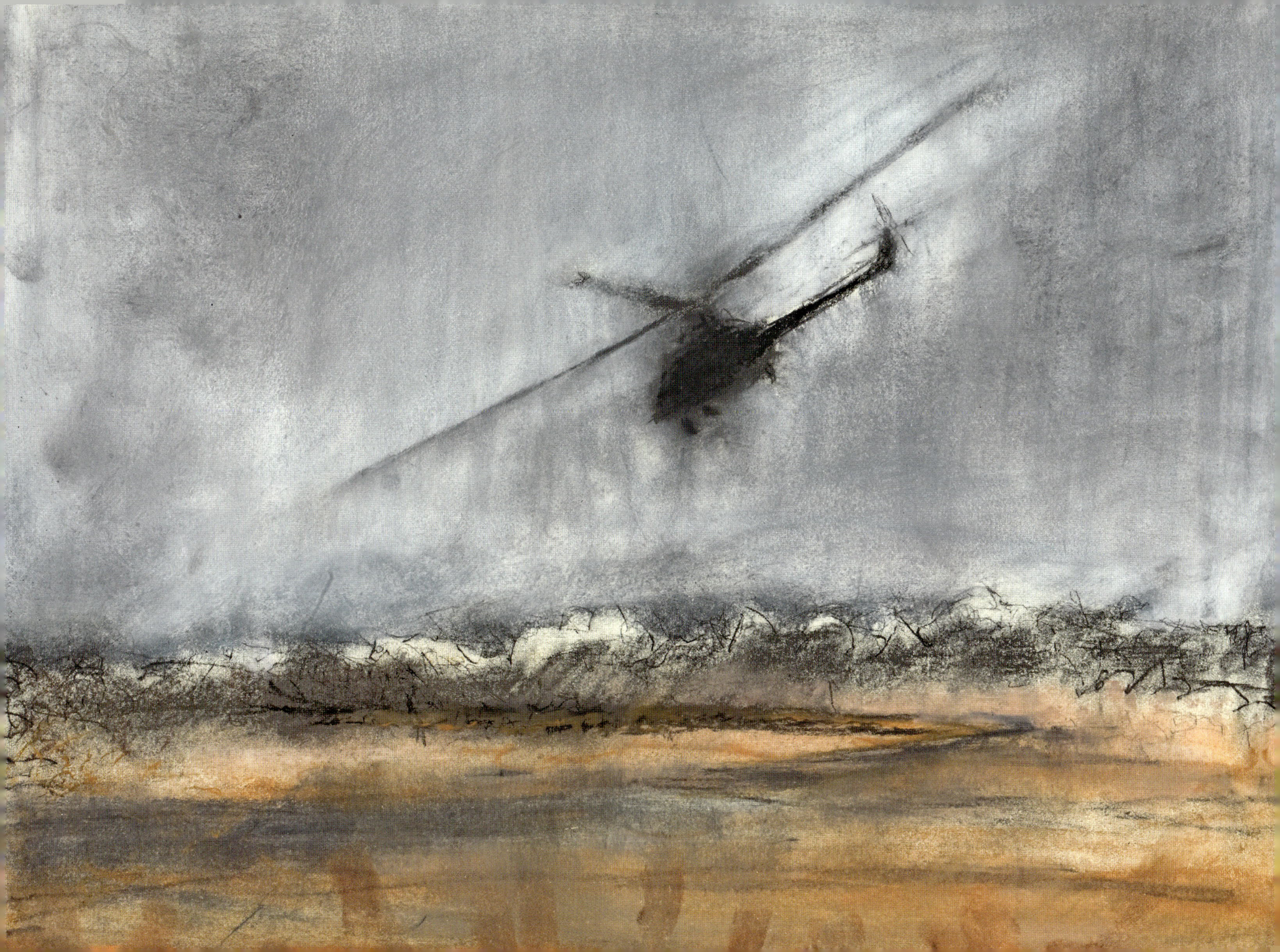

 Terrain II, 2004

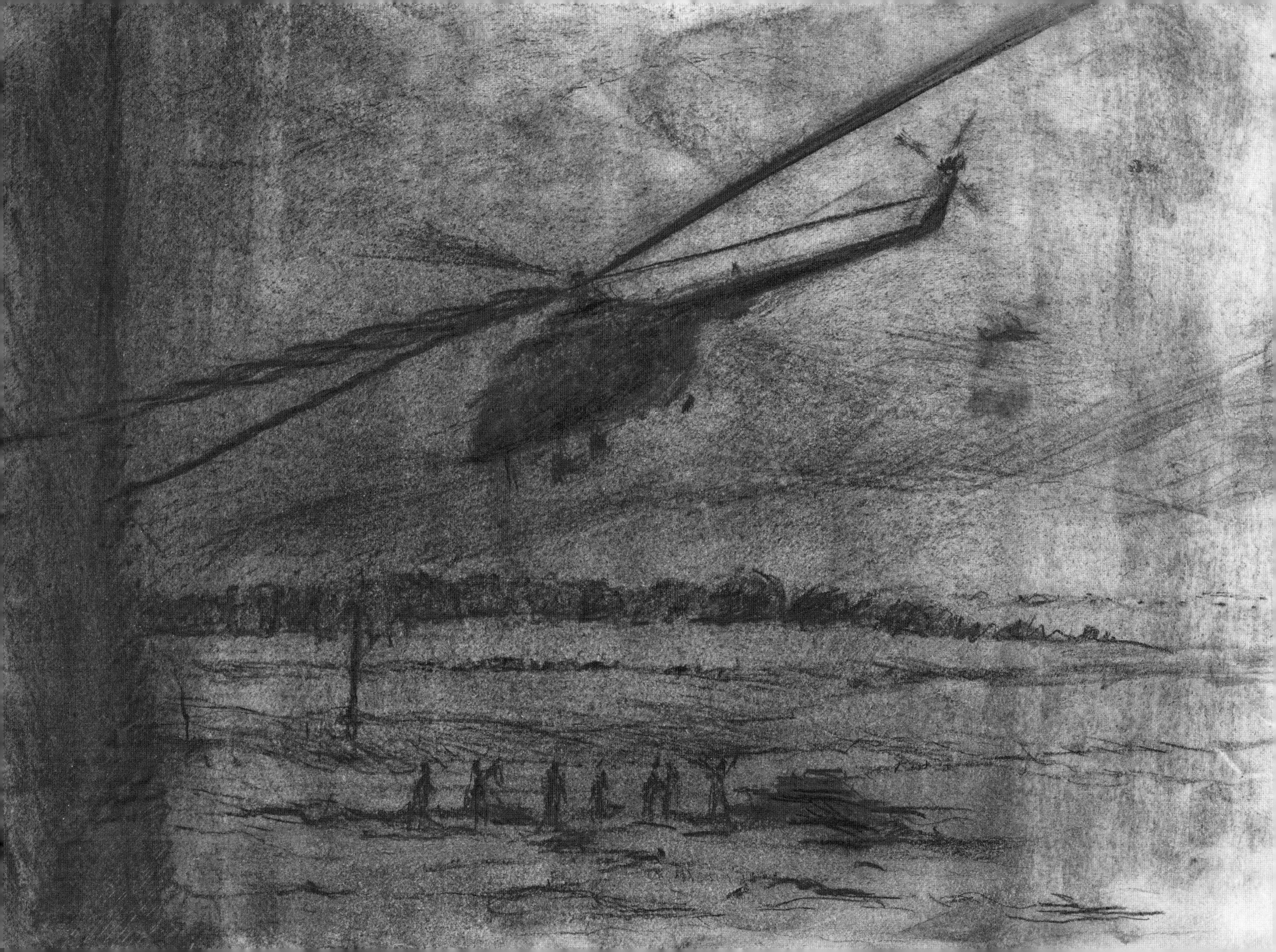

71 Nightflight, 2010

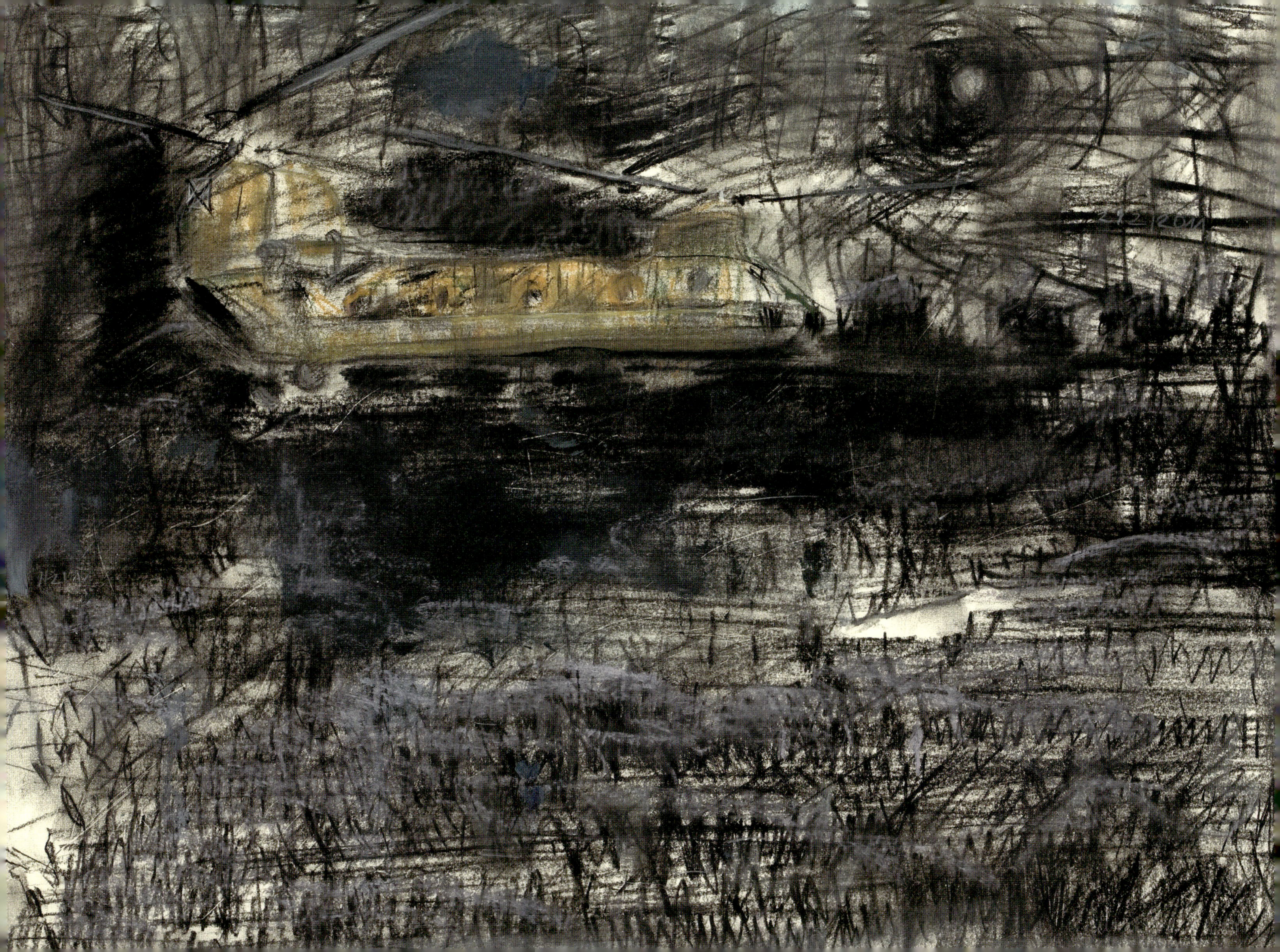

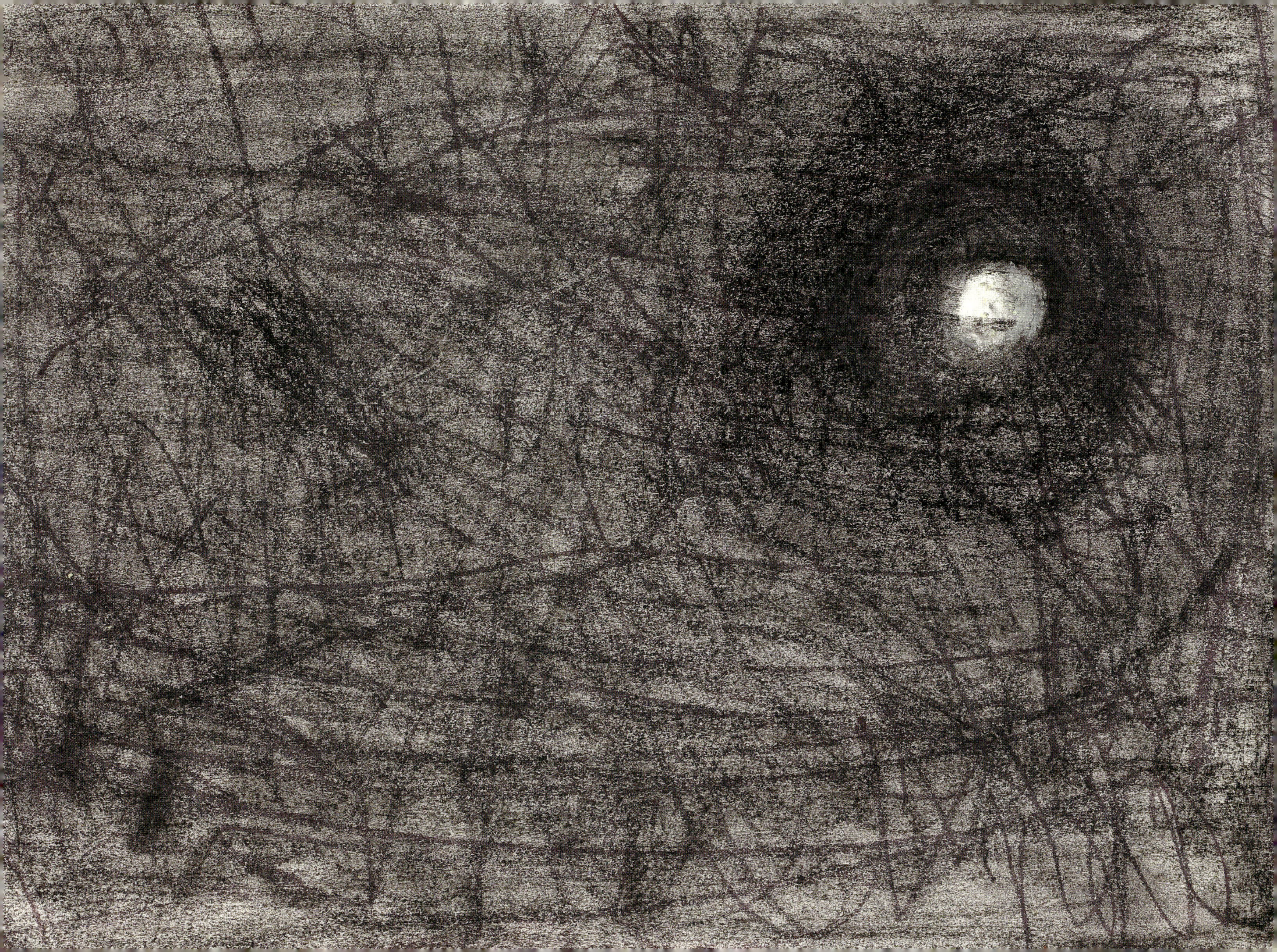

List of Works

1 Abend I / *Evening I*
2007
42 x 56 cm
Charcoal and pastel on paper

2 Abend II / *Evening II*
2009
42 x 56 cm
Charcoal and pastel on paper

3 Start Nacht / *Start Night*
2004
30 x 40 cm
Charcoal on paper

4 Start Tag / Start *Day*
2004
30 x 40 cm
Charcoal on paper

5 Kandahar
2004
52 x 57 cm
Oil on canvas

6 Rettung (Flut) / *Saving Action (Flood)*
2004
30 x 40cm
Charcoal and pastel on paper

7 Flut / *Flood*
2004
41 x 51 cm
Oil on canvas

8 Bagdad / *Baghdad*
2004
30 x 40 cm
Charcoal on paper

9 Bagdad II / *Baghdad II*
2003
40 x 30 cm
Charcoal on paper

10 Notlandung I / *Crash Landing I*
2004
30 x 40 cm
Charcoal and pastel on paper

11 Notlandung II / *Crash Landing II*
2004
30 x 40 cm
Charcoal and pastel on paper

12 Notlandung III / *Crash Landing III*
2004
30 x 40 cm
Charcoal and pastel on paper

13 Notlandung IV / *Crash Landing IV*
2004
30 x 40 cm
Charcoal and pastel on paper

14 Notlandung V / *Crash Landing V*
2004
30 x 40 cm
Charcoal and pastel on paper

15 Notlandung / *Crash Landing*
2004
80 x 100 cm
Oil on canvas

16 Flucht / *Flight*
2006
24 x 32 cm
Charcoal on paper

17 Überwachung II / *Surveillance II*
2003
30 x 40 cm
Charcaol and pencil on paper

18 Überwachung III / *Surveillance III*
2003
30 x 40 cm
Charcaol and pencil on paper

19 Überwachung I / *Surveillance I*
2003
30 x 40 cm
Charcaol and pencil on paper

20 Dust
2008
60 x 70 cm
Oil on canvas

21 Soviet
2012
30 x 40 cm
Charcoal, oil crayon and pastel on paper

22 Sibirien / *Siberia*
2012
42 x 56 cm
Charcoal, oil, oil crayon and pastel on paper

23 Aurora I
2006
100 x 120 cm
Oil on canvas

24 Des Morgens / *In the Morning*
2010
70 x 90 cm
Oil on canvas

25 Abendphantasie / *Evening Fantasy*
2010
120 x 90 cm
Oil on canvas

26 Grau / *Grey*
2012
30 x 40 cm
Charcoal, oil crayon and pastel on paper

27 Blau / *Blue*
2010
30 x 40 cm
Charcoal, pastel and oil crayon on paper

28 Grün / *Green*
2010
30 x 40 cm
Charcoal and pastel on paper

29 Rosa / *Pink*
2010
30 x 40 cm
Charcoal, pastel and oil crayon on paper

30 Abschied / *Farewell*
2012
30 x 40 cm
Charcoal, oil crayon and pastel on paper

31 Mother
2010
60 x 55 cm
Oil on canvas

32 Macbeth
2005
42 x 62 cm
Oil on paper

33 Kinshasa
2004
50 x 70 cm
Oil on canvas

34 Parade (Skizze)
2006
24 x 32 cm
Charcoal and oil crayon
on paper

35 Parade II
2010
80 x 120 cm
Oil on canvas

36 Parade I
2007
100 x 120 cm
Oil on canvas

37 Attack
2009
65 x 75 cm
Oil on canvas

38 Dschungel / *Jungle*
2010
42 x 56 cm
Charcoal, oil crayon
and pastel on paper

39 Deadline
2004
42 x 56 cm
Charcoal, oil crayon
and pastel on paper

40 Battlefield
2012
30 x 40 cm
Charcoal and pastel
on paper

41 Sea Sprite
2009
50 x 55 cm
Oil on canvas

42 Blauer Helikopter /
Blue Helicopter
2010
42 x 56 cm
Charcoal, oil crayon
and pastel on paper

43 Marine / *Marine*
2009
42 x 56 cm
Charcoal, oil crayon
and pastel on paper

44 Weiß / *White*
2009
30 x40 cm
Charcoal, oil crayon
and pastel on paper

45 Meer II / *Ocean II*
2004
42 x 56 cm
Charcoal, pastel and
oil crayon on paper

46 Meer I / *Ocean I*
2004
42 x 56 cm
Charcoal and pastel
on paper

47 Übung I / *Training I*
2004
30 x 40 cm
Charcoal, pastel and
oil crayon on paper

48 Übung II / *Training II*
2004
42 x 56 cm
Charcoal, pastel and
oil crayon on paper

49 Test
2005
50 x 60 cm
Oil on canvas

50 N.Y.
2007
30 x 40 cm
Charcoal and pastel
on paper

51 Schöner Helikopter I /
Beautiful Helicopter I
2009
24 x 32 cm
Charcoal and oil on paper

52 Schöner Helikopter II /
Beautiful Helicopter II
2009
24 x 32 cm
Charcoal and oil on paper

53 Schwarz / *Black*
2009
30 x 40 cm
Charcoal, pastel and
oil crayon on paper

54 Waldhubschrauber VI
2006
24 x 32 cm
Charcoal, pastel and
oil crayon on paper

55 Waldhubschrauber III
2006
24 x 32 cm
Charcoal, pastel and
oil crayon on paper

56 Waldhubschrauber II
2006
24 x 32 cm
Charcoal, pastel and
oil crayon on paper

57 Waldhubschrauber I
2006
24 x32 cm
Charcoal, pastel and
oil crayon on paper

58 Botschaft / *Embassy*
2004
30 x 40 cm
Charcoal, pastel and
oil crayon on paper

59 Grenzstation / *Border Checkpoint*
2011
40 x 30 cm
Charcoal, oil crayon
and pastel on paper

60 Grenze / *Border*
2013
58 x 72 cm
Oil on canvas

61 Eiswand / *Ice Wall*
2011
70 x 90 cm
Oil on canvas

62 Nordpol I /
North Pole I
2004
56 x 42 cm
Charcoal on paper

63 Nordpol II /
North Pole II
2004
56 x 42 cm
Charcoal and pastel
on paper

64 North Pole
2005
50 x 60 cm
Oil on canvas

65 Sea King
(detail)
2007
80 x 120 cm
Oil on canvas

66 Sea King (Rain)
2013
30 x 40 cm
Charcoal and pastel
on paper

67 Rescue
2013
42 x 56 cm
Charcoal oil crayon
and pastel on paper

68 Gelände III / *Terrain III*
2009
30 x 40 cm
Pastel, charcaol, and
gouche on paper

69 Gelände I / *Terrain I*
2004
30 x 40 cm
Charcoal and pastel
on paper

70 Gelände II / *Terrain II*
2004
30 x 40 cm
Charcoal and pastel
on paper

71 Nachtflug / *Nightflight*
2010
30 x 40 cm
Charcoal and pastel
on paper

72 Mond / *Moon*
2011
30 x 40 cm
Charcoal on paper

Cover
Kapitulation / *Surrender*
(detail)
2012
30 x 40 cm
Charcoal on paper

'In the Morning' and 'Evening Fantasy' are taken from "Friedrich Hölderlin: Poems and Fragments" translated by Michael Hamburger. Published by Anvil Press Poetry; fourth edition in 2004

Design: *Sabine Pflitsch (probsteibooks)*
Proofreading: *Sandra Rehme*
Translation from the Polish:
Antonia Lloyd-Jones
Translation from the German:
Fiona Elliott (Hans Ulrich Obrist)
Production:
Printmanagement Plitt, Oberhausen

Set using Avenir on Symbol Tatami.

First published by Heni Publishing London

A catalogue record for this book is available from the British Library.

ISBN 978-0-9930103-0-9

Printed in Germany

Special thanks to Adam Zagajewski who wrote his poem for this book.